Pearson Edexcel GCSE (9-1) Combined Science Lab Book

Contents

CB1b	Core practical 1: Looking at cells	2
CB1g	Core practical 2: pH and enzymes	8
CB1h	Core practical 4: Osmosis in potato slices	13
CB6b	Core practical 6: Light intensity and photosynthesis	18
CB8d	Core practical 7: Respiration rates	22
CB9b	Core practical 8: Quadrats and transects	26
CC2d	Core practical 1: Investigating inks	30
CC8c	Core practical 3: Preparing copper sulfate	38
CC8d	Core practical 2: Investigating neutralisation	42
CC10a	Core practical 4: Electrolysis of copper sulfate solution	46
CC14a & b	Core practical 6: Investigating reaction rates	51
CP2d	Core practical 1: Investigating acceleration	60
CP4b	Core practical 2: Investigating waves	64
CP5a	Core practical 3: Investigating refraction	70
CP9e	Core practical 5: Investigating resistance	74
CP12a	Core practical 6: Investigating densities	81
CP12b & c	Core practical 7: Investigating water	84
CP13a	Core practical 8: Investigating springs	90
	Equations	95
	Glossary	97
	Answers	98

Published by Pearson Education Limited, 80 Strand, London, WC2R 0RL.
www.pearsonschoolsandfecolleges.co.uk

Copies of official specifications for all Pearson Edexcel qualifications may be found on the website: qualifications.pearson.com

Text © Mark Levesley, Penny Johnson, Sue Kearsey, Iain Brand, Nigel Saunders, Sue Robilliard, Carol Tear and Pearson Education Ltd 2018.
Series Editor: Mark Levesley
Designed by Pete Stratton, Pearson Education Ltd
Edited by Haremi Ltd
Typeset by Servis Filmsetting Ltd
Original illustrations © Pearson Education Ltd 2018
Cover design by Pete Stratton
Cover photo/illustration © Fotolia: mgs

First published 2017
Second edition 2018

19 18
10 9 8 7 6 5 4 3 2 1

British Library Cataloguing in Publication Data
A catalogue record for this book is available from the British Library
ISBN 9781292267869

Copyright notice
All rights reserved. No part of this publication may be reproduced in any form or by any means (including photocopying or storing it in any medium by electronic means and whether or not transiently or incidentally to some other use of this publication) without the written permission of the copyright owner, except in accordance with the provisions of the Copyright, Designs and Patents Act 1988 or under the terms of a licence issued by the Copyright Licensing Agency, Barnards Inn, 86 Fetter Lane, London EC4A 1EN (www.cla.co.uk). Applications for the copyright owner's written permission should be addressed to the publisher.

All other media © Pearson Education Ltd

Printed in Italy by L.E.G.O. S.p.A

Acknowledgements
The publishers would like to thank Ian Gouge, Chris Shipley and Chris Jones for their contributions to this resource and would like to thank Alison Court and John Kavanagh for their contributions to the previous edition.
The rights of Mark Levesley, Penny Johnson, Sue Kearsey, Iain Brand, Nigel Saunders, Sue Robilliard and Carol Tear to be identified as authors of this work have been asserted by them in accordance with the Copyright, Designs and Patents Act 1988.
The publishers would also like to thank Pearson Edexcel for allowing them the use of exam question 3(b) from Physics Paper 2 (1PH0/2F) of Level 1/Level 2 GCSE (9-1), Foundation Tier, 2017.

Edexcel GCSE (9–1)
Combined Science

CB1b — Core practical 1: Looking at cells

Examining specimens using a microscope and then making labelled drawings of them is a basic skill that you will need in your study of biology. This practical gives you an opportunity to practise this skill.

Your teacher may watch to see if you can:
- handle microscopes and slides carefully and safely.

Method 1: Examining pre-prepared slides of cells

A You will be changing the magnification of your microscope during this section of the practical. Use the box below to record all of your calculations. Set up your microscope on the lowest magnification objective lens. Work out the total magnification and measure the diameter of the field of view (by using the microscope to observe a transparent ruler).

B Put the next most powerful objective lens in place. Work out the magnification and by how much it has increased from the magnification in step **A** (e.g. moving from a ×10 to a ×50 is an increase of 5 times). Now divide the diameter of the field of view from step **A** by the increase in magnification to give you the new diameter of the field of view (e.g. if the field of view in step **A** was 2 mm, then 2 ÷ 5 = 0.4 mm). Do this for each objective lens. Record the total magnification and field of view diameter for each objective lens.

Practical Objective
To use a microscope to observe cells and sub-cellular structures.

Apparatus
- light microscope
- lamp
- prepared slides
- transparent ruler

Safety
- Handle slides with care.

C Now go back to the lowest magnification objective lens and observe a prepared slide.

D Use higher magnifications to observe the cells. Estimate the sizes using your field of view diameters.

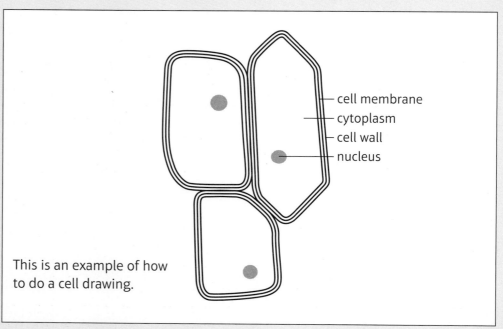

This is an example of how to do a cell drawing.

Labels: cell membrane, cytoplasm, cell wall, nucleus

Edexcel GCSE (9–1)
Combined Science

CB1b Core practical 1: Looking at cells

E Using a sharp pencil, draw 4–5 cells in the box below. There is an example of how to do a microscope drawing in the box on the previous page. Identify and label the cells' parts. Use a ruler to draw your label lines. Write on the magnification. Add any sizes that you have estimated. Have a look for mitochondria (you may not find any as they are very difficult to see).

Edexcel GCSE (9–1)
Combined Science

CB1b — Core practical 1: Looking at cells

Method 2: Examining your cheek cells

A Using the pipette, add a small drop of water to the slide.

B Stroke the inside of your cheek gently with the wooden spatula. You only want to collect loose cells, so do not scratch the inside of your mouth.

C Use the end of the spatula that has been in your mouth to stir the drop of water on the slide. Place the used spatula in disinfectant.

D Put on gloves and use a pipette to add a small drop of methylene blue solution. This makes cells easier to see.

E Place a coverslip onto the slide at a 45° angle on one edge of the drop. Then use a toothpick to gently lower the coverslip down onto the drop, as shown in the diagram. Avoid trapping air bubbles, which appear as black-edged circles under a microscope.

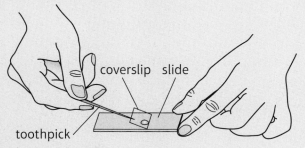

F Touch a piece of paper towel to any liquid that spreads out from under the coverslip.

G Use the lowest magnification objective lens to observe the slide. The nuclei of the cheek cells will be dark blue.

H Use higher magnifications to observe the cells. Estimate the sizes using your field of view diameters.

I Using a sharp pencil, draw 4–5 cells in the box below. Identify and label the cells' parts. Use a ruler to draw your label lines. Write on the magnification. Add any sizes that you have estimated. Have a look for mitochondria (you may not find any as they are very difficult to see).

Apparatus
- eye protection
- light microscope
- lamp
- microscope slide
- coverslip
- methylene blue solution
- pipette
- paper towel
- water
- gloves
- wooden toothpick/ cocktail stick
- sterile wooden spatula/ tongue depressor
- disinfectant

Safety
- Wear eye protection.
- Handle slides with care.
- Anything that you have put into your mouth should be placed in disinfectant after use.
- Wear gloves if using solutions that may stain.

Edexcel GCSE (9–1)
Combined Science

CB1b — Core practical 1: Looking at cells

Method 3: Examining onion or rhubarb stem cells

A If you are going to look at onion cells, put on gloves and use a pipette to add a drop of iodine solution to a microscope slide. If you are going to look at rhubarb, add a drop of water to a microscope slide.

B Using forceps, remove a very small piece of the thin 'skin' on the inside of the fleshy part of the onion. It is very thin indeed and quite tricky to handle. Or remove a thin piece of red 'skin' from a rhubarb stem.

C Place the small piece of skin on the drop on the slide.

D Place a coverslip onto the slide at a 45° angle on one edge of the drop. Then use a toothpick to gently lower the coverslip down onto the drop, as shown in the diagram. Avoid trapping air bubbles, which appear as black-edged circles under a microscope.

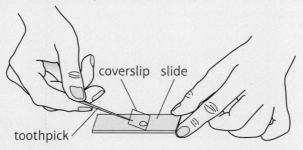

E Touch a piece of paper towel to any liquid that spreads out from under the coverslip.

F Use the lowest magnification objective lens to observe the slide. Then use higher magnifications to observe the cells in more detail. Estimate sizes as you observe.

G Using a sharp pencil, draw 4–5 cells in the box below. Identify the cells' parts and label them. Use a ruler to draw your label lines. Write on the magnification. Add any sizes that you have estimated. Have a look for mitochondria (you may not find any as they are very difficult to see).

Apparatus
- eye protection
- light microscope
- lamp
- microscope slide
- coverslip
- iodine solution
- pipette
- paper towel
- water
- forceps
- wooden toothpick
- piece of onion bulb or rhubarb stem
- gloves

Safety
- Wear eye protection.
- Handle slides and microscopes with care.
- Wear gloves if using solutions that may stain.

Edexcel GCSE (9–1)
Combined Science

CB1b Core practical 1: Looking at cells

Method 4: Examining pondweed

A Tear off a very small piece of pondweed leaf: a square with sides of up to 2 mm.

B Place the leaf sample onto a microscope slide and add a drop of water.

C Place a coverslip onto the slide at a 45° angle on one edge of the drop. Then use a toothpick to gently lower the coverslip down onto the drop, as shown in the diagram on the previous page. Avoid trapping air bubbles, which appear as black-edged circles under a microscope.

D Touch a piece of paper towel to any liquid that spreads out from under the coverslip.

E Use the lowest magnification objective lens to observe the slide.

F Use higher magnifications to observe the cells in more detail. Estimate sizes as you observe.

G Using a sharp pencil, draw 4–5 cells in the box below. Identify the cells' parts and label them. Use a ruler to draw your label lines. Write on the magnification. Add any sizes that you have estimated. If you watch very carefully when you have the cells under a high magnification, you may well see the chloroplasts moving as the cytoplasm moves inside the cells.

Apparatus

- eye protection
- light microscope
- lamp
- microscope slide
- coverslip
- pipette
- paper towel
- water
- forceps
- wooden toothpick
- piece of pondweed

Safety

- Wear eye protection.
- Handle slides and microscopes with care.

Edexcel GCSE (9–1)
Combined Science

CB1b Core practical 1: Looking at cells

Exam-style questions

1 A microscope is fitted with three objective lenses (of ×2, ×5 and ×10).

  a State what ×2 on a lens means. (1)

  b The microscope has a ×7 eyepiece lens. Calculate the possible total magnifications. Show your working. (3)

2 A student wanted to observe dividing cells.
The student carefully squashed the root tip of an onion plant onto a microscope slide and used a pipette to add a small drop of iodine solution.
Describe how the student should use a light microscope to view the prepared root tip. (3)

3 Sasha observes palisade cells from a star anise plant at magnification ×400.
The length of one palisade cell is 0.80 mm.
Calculate the length of the cell in µm. (2)

_____ µm

Edexcel GCSE (9–1)
Combined Science

CB1g Core practical 2: pH and enzymes

Amylase is an enzyme made in the salivary glands in your mouth and in the pancreas. It catalyses the breakdown of starch into smaller sugar molecules. The iodine test identifies the presence of starch, but does not react with sugar. You will use this test to show how effective amylase is in digesting starch at different pHs.

Your teacher may watch to see if you can:
- work safely
- collect accurate data.

Method

A Drop one drop of iodine solution into each depression of the dimple tile.

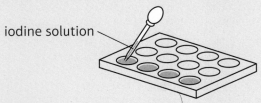

B Measure 2 cm³ of amylase solution into a test tube using a syringe.

C Add 1 cm³ of your pH solution to the test tube using a second syringe. Record the pH of the solution that you are using.

D Using a third syringe, add 2 cm³ starch solution to the mixture and start the stop clock. Use the pipette to stir the mixture.

E After 20 seconds, take a small amount of the mixture in the pipette and place one drop of it on the first iodine drop on the tile. Return the rest of the solution in the pipette to the test tube.

F If the iodine solution turns black, then there is still starch in the mixture and you should repeat step **E** (after 10 seconds). If it remains yellow, then all the starch is digested and you should record the time taken for this to happen.

G If there is time, repeat the experiment using a solution of different pH for step **C**.

Prediction

1 Predict at which pH the amylase will digest starch fastest. Explain your prediction. Record your prediction and explanation in the box below.

Practical Objective
To investigate the effect of pH on the rate of digestion of starch by amylase.

Apparatus
- eye protection
- iodine solution in dropping bottle
- dimple tile
- test tubes
- test-tube rack
- syringes
- pipette
- amylase solution
- starch solution
- solutions of specific pH
- stop clock

Safety
- Eye protection should be worn.

Edexcel GCSE (9-1)
Combined Science

CB1g Core practical 2: pH and enzymes

Recording your results

2 Draw a table in the box below, to present these results clearly.

3 Collect data from all the groups in the class so that you have results for each of the different pHs. If you have more than one result for each pH, calculate a mean time for each one. Record the mean times in the box below.

Considering your results

4 Using the graph paper below, plot a line graph to show the time taken for amylase to digest starch with the different pHs.

Edexcel GCSE (9–1)
Combined Science

CB1g — Core practical 2: pH and enzymes

5 Look at your graph and use it to describe the effect of pH on the time taken for amylase to digest starch.

6 Suggest a reason for the shape of your graph.

Evaluation

7 Describe any problems you had with carrying out the experiment.

8 Suggest reasons for the problems and how the method could be changed to help reduce the problems.

9 Were any of the results surprising? If so, why?

10 Do you think you have enough results to support your conclusion? Explain your answer.

Edexcel GCSE (9–1)
Combined Science

CB1g Core practical 2: pH and enzymes

Exam-style questions

1 Catalase is an enzyme that breaks down hydrogen peroxide into water and oxygen. Some students are investigating the effect of pH on this enzyme-controlled reaction by collecting the oxygen. One suggestion is to bubble the gas through water and collect it in an upturned measuring cylinder full of water. Another suggestion is to collect the water in a gas syringe.

    a Explain which method of gas collection you would use. (2)

    b Explain how the students should measure the pH in their investigation. (2)

    c The table shows the results from the students' investigation. Draw a graph to display the results.

Time (min)	Volume of O_2 released (cm^3)	
	at pH 3	at pH 6
1	1.4	1.6
2	2.7	3.2
3	4.2	5.6
4	5.9	5.7
5	6.6	8.4
6	8.4	10.6

(3)

Edexcel GCSE (9–1)
Combined Science

CB1g Core practical 2: pH and enzymes

d Identify the anomalous result and suggest a reason for the error. (2)

e Calculate the average rate of reaction (average volume of oxygen produced per minute) at pH 6. (1)

2 Scientists working on bioleaching are interested in an enzyme called glucose oxidase, which is found in many microorganisms. The graph shows the results from an investigation into the effect of pH on the rate of activity of glucose oxidase from two different types of bacteria.

a What is the optimum pH for glucose oxidase from each type of bacterium? (2)

b Explain which enzyme is more active at pH 5. (2)

c Most mine water is acidic. Explain which bacterium might be more useful for bioleaching mine water. (2)

Edexcel GCSE (9–1)
Combined Science

CB1h — Core practical 4: Osmosis in potato slices

Osmosis is the overall movement of water molecules through a semi-permeable membrane from a region where there are more water molecules in a particular volume to a region where there are fewer, through a semi-permeable membrane. The cells in a potato contain many substances dissolved in water. The cells are surrounded by cell membranes that are permeable to water. When a strip of potato is placed in a solution, the overall movement of water molecules between the potato cells and the solution will depend on which has the higher concentration of solutes. In this practical, you will investigate osmosis in potato strips in terms of the percentage change in mass of potato in different solutions.

Your teacher may watch to see if you can:
- measure accurately
- work carefully.

Practical Objective
To investigate how solution concentration affects percentage change in mass of potato strips due to osmosis.

Apparatus
- four potato strips
- accurate balance
- four boiling tubes and rack (or beakers)
- waterproof pen
- four sucrose solutions: 0%, 40%, 80%, 100%
- forceps
- paper towels

Safety
- Do not drink any of the solutions or eat the potatoes.

Method

A Using the waterproof pen, label each tube with the name of one of the solutions. Place the boiling tubes in the rack.

B Dry a potato strip carefully by blotting it with a paper towel. The potato strips can be removed using a cork borer, as shown in the diagram, or cut using a scalpel. This will have been done for you, before the experiment. Measure the mass of the potato strip using the balance.

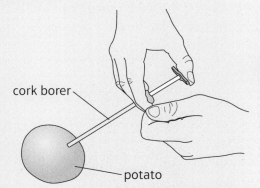

C Place the potato strip into one of the tubes. Record the label on the tube and the mass of the strip in your results table (see next page).

D Repeat steps **B** and **C** until all strips have been measured and placed in tubes.

E Carefully fill each tube with the appropriate solution, so that the potato is fully covered. Leave the tubes for at least 15 minutes.

F For each potato strip, use the forceps to remove it from its tube, blot dry on a paper towel and measure its mass again. Record all the masses in the results table.

Prediction

1. For each of the four solutions you will use, predict whether the potato strips will gain mass, lose mass or keep the same mass. Explain your predictions. Record your predictions and explanations in the box below.

_____
_____
_____
_____
_____
_____
_____

Edexcel GCSE (9–1)
Combined Science

CB1h — Core practical 4: Osmosis in potato slices

Recording your results

2. Complete the first three columns of the table below, labelled 'Solution', **A** and **B**, with the solution descriptions and your measurements from the experiment.

Solution	A Mass of potato strip at start (g)	B Mass of potato strip at end (g)	C Change in mass (g) = B – A	D % change in mass = $\frac{C}{A} \times 100\%$

3. Complete column **C** by calculating the change in mass for each potato strip using the formula shown.
4. Complete column **D** by calculating the percentage change in mass for each potato strip using the formula shown.
5. Compare the results for percentage change in mass from all groups in the class for each solution. Identify any results that seem very different from the others (anomalous results).
   Try to suggest a reason why they are so different.

_____

6. Using all results except the anomalous one(s), calculate a mean value for percentage change in mass for each solution.

Edexcel GCSE (9–1)
Combined Science

CB1h — Core practical 4: Osmosis in potato slices

7 Draw a suitable chart or graph to show the mean percentage change in the mass of each potato strip on the *y*-axis against the solution description on the *x*-axis.

Considering your results/conclusions

8 Describe the pattern shown in your chart or graph.

9 Explain the pattern shown in your chart or graph, using the word 'osmosis' in your answer.

10 Explain why you calculated percentage change in mass.

11 Explain why calculating a mean value from several repeats of the same experiment is more likely to give a value that can be reproduced by others.

Edexcel GCSE (9–1)
Combined Science

CB1h Core practical 4: Osmosis in potato slices

Evaluation

12 Describe any problems that you had with the experiment. Suggest how these could be reduced or avoided to produce better results.

Exam-style questions

1 The table shows the results from an experiment similar to the one described in the method.

Tube	A	B	C	D
Sucrose concentration (%)	0	10	30	50
Mass of potato at start (g)	4.81	5.22	4.94	4.86
Mass of potato at end (g)	4.90	4.96	4.39	3.69

a For each solution, calculate the gain or loss in mass of the potato piece. (2)

b For each solution, calculate the percentage change in mass of the potato. (2)

c Give a reason for the result from tube A. (1)

d Explain the results for tubes B–D. (2)

Edexcel GCSE (9–1)
Combined Science

CB1h Core practical 4: Osmosis in potato slices

e Use the results to give the possible solute concentration of potato tissue, giving a reason for your answer. (2)

f Describe how the method could be adapted to give a more accurate answer to part **e**. (1)

2 The graph below shows the results of an experiment comparing osmosis in tissue from a halophyte plant and a potato in the same solution.

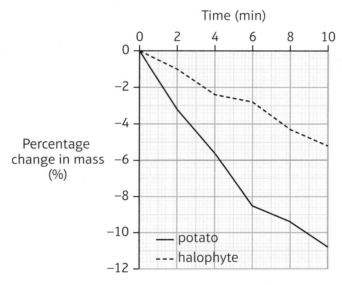

a Identify, with a reason, which tissue lost water faster over the first 5 minutes. (2)

b Explain why it lost water faster than the other tissue. (2)

c Calculate the average rate of change in mass over the first four minutes for the potato. (1)

Edexcel GCSE (9–1) Combined Science

CB6b Core practical 6: Light intensity and photosynthesis

Introduction
Microscopic algae have cells that contain chloroplasts, like plant leaf cells. The algae can be trapped in jelly balls to make them easier to handle. You will put algal balls in an indicator that changes colour as carbon dioxide levels change. Under normal conditions the indicator is a red colour, but this changes to yellow at higher carbon dioxide concentrations and purple at lower carbon dioxide concentrations.

Your teacher may watch to see if you can:
- follow instructions carefully
- work safely.

Method
A Decide the different distances you are going to use between the algae and the lamp. For each distance you will need one clear glass bottle. You will also need one extra bottle.

B Add 20 algal balls to each bottle.

C Add the same volume of indicator solution to each bottle and put on the bottle caps.

D Your teacher will have a chart or a range of bottles showing the colours of the indicator at different pHs. Compare the colour in your bottles with this pH range to work out the pH at the start.

E Set up a heat filter between the lamp and where you will place your tubes. The heat filter is a water-filled bottle or other clear container. Take great care not to spill water near the lamp.

F Cover one bottle in kitchen foil, so that it is in the dark.

G Place your bottles at measured distances from the lamp. Put the bottle covered in kitchen foil next to the bottle that is closest to the lamp.

H Turn on the lamp and time 60 minutes (or longer).

I Compare the colours of all your bottles with those of the pH range bottles (or chart).

J Record the pHs of the solutions in your bottles in a suitable table.

K For each bottle, calculate the change in pH per hour. Add these calculations to your table.

Practical Objective
To find out how light intensity affects the rate of photosynthesis.

Apparatus
- eye protection
- bijou bottles and caps
- beaker of algal balls
- hydrogen carbonate indicator
- lamp and heat filter
- metre rule
- measuring cylinder
- kitchen foil
- clock/stop clock/watch
- plastic forceps/spoon

Safety
- Wear eye protection.
- Wash your hands after setting up the experiment.
- Avoid touching the hot lamp.

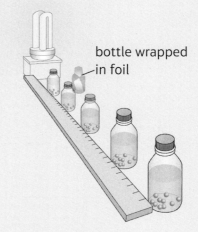

bottle wrapped in foil

Recording your results
1 Record your results in this table.

Distance from lamp to bottle (cm)	pH at start	pH at end	Rate of photosynthesis (change in pH/hour)

Edexcel GCSE (9–1) Combined Science

CB6b — Core practical 6: Light intensity and photosynthesis

Considering your results/conclusions

2 a For each bottle, calculate the rate of photosynthesis as the change in pH per hour.

change in pH = pH at end − pH at start

$$\text{rate} = \frac{\text{change in pH}}{\text{time (in hours)}}$$

b Use your calculations to complete the last column of the table on the previous page.

3 Plot your results on a graph. Plot the variable that you have changed (the independent variable) on the horizontal axis. Plot the rate of photosynthesis on the vertical axis.

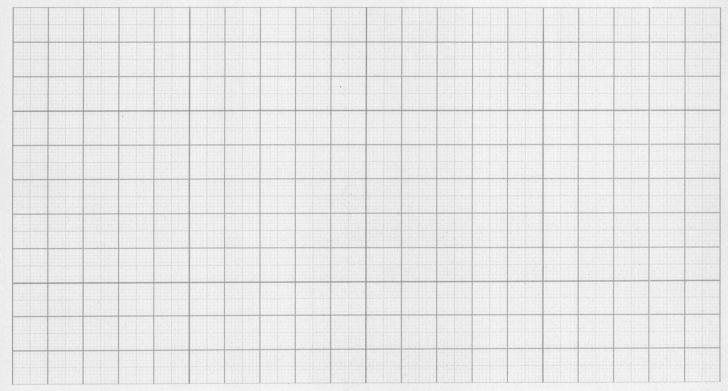

4 a Describe the pattern shown on your graph.

b Explain why this pattern is observed.

Evaluation

5 Fill in the missing words in the sentences below to explain the point of the bottle covered in foil.

The part of an experiment in which the _____ variable is not applied is called the control. A control is used to check that the _____ variable has an effect (and that the effect is not due to another variable). In this experiment, the independent variable is the _____ intensity. The control is the _____. We know that the independent variable has a direct effect on the final pH of the indicator because _____ _____.

Edexcel GCSE (9–1)
Combined Science

CB6b — Core practical 6: Light intensity and photosynthesis

Exam-style question

1 Pondweed was placed in a sealed tank of water with an oxygen probe. A datalogger recorded the oxygen concentration in the water. During the experiment, a lamp was switched on and then off again. The results are shown in the graph.

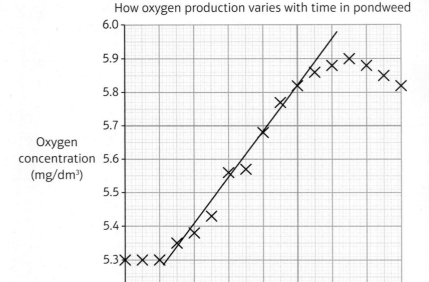

How oxygen production varies with time in pondweed

a Suggest at what time the lamp was switched on. Give a reason for your answer. **(1)**

b Suggest at what time the lamp was switched off. Give a reason for your answer. **(1)**

c The slope (or gradient), *m*, of the line of best fit shows the rate of photosynthesis. Use the graph to calculate the average rate of photosynthesis indicated by the slope on the graph. Show all your working. **(3)**

Edexcel GCSE (9–1)
Combined Science

CB6b Core practical 6: Light intensity and photosynthesis

d The linear relationship shown by the line of best fit can be shown by $y = mx + c$. For this graph, $c = 5.1$. Calculate the concentration of oxygen after 4 minutes 20 seconds. (3)

e A student thinks the line will be steeper if the light intensity is increased. Explain why the student thinks this. (3)

f The idea is tested, but the steepness of the line does not change. Suggest a reason for this. (2)

g State one other possible way of increasing the steepness of the line. (1)

Edexcel GCSE (9–1) Combined Science

CB8d Core practical 7: Respiration rates

Considering your results/conclusions

2 Plot your results on a graph.

3 a What was the independent variable in this investigation?

b What was the dependent variable?

c State one control variable described in the method.

d Explain why the variable you gave in **c** needs to be controlled.

e Describe the relationship between the temperature and rate of aerobic respiration.

Edexcel GCSE (9–1)
Combined Science

CB8d — Core practical 7: Respiration rates

f Suggest an explanation for this relationship. (*Hint:* think about the effect of temperature on chemical reactions.)

Evaluation

4 The organisms in the tube are respiring aerobically.

   a What gas are they using up?

   b What gas are they producing?

   c Explain why the gas you named in **b** does not collect in the tube.

Exam-style questions

1 State the lowest and the highest temperature at which you would test the respiration rate in small organisms. Give reasons for your choices. (2)

2 The table shows the results of one experiment to measure the effect of temperature on the respiration rate of waxworms.

Temperature (°C)	Distance moved by the coloured liquid in 5 min (mm)
10	9
10	9
10	10
15	12
15	15
15	13
20	17
20	20
20	18
25	25
25	25
25	28
30	10
30	33
30	38

24

Edexcel GCSE (9–1)
Combined Science

CB8d Core practical 7: Respiration rates

a Explain why the measurements were repeated for each temperature. (1)

b Plot all the results on a graph. (2)

c Identify the anomalous result. (1)

d Suggest an explanation for this anomalous result. (1)

e Draw a line of best fit through the remaining points. (1)
f Describe the correlation shown in your diagram. (1)

g Suggest an explanation for this correlation. (2)

Edexcel GCSE (9–1)
Combined Science

CB9b — Core practical 8: Quadrats and transects

A transect is used to study the distribution of organisms and how it is affected by changes in environmental conditions. With a belt transect, quadrats are placed at regular intervals along the transect line to sample the organisms.

Your teacher may watch to see if you can:
- work efficiently
- follow safety guidance.

Method

A If your teacher has not told you where to place the transect, look for somewhere that shows obvious variation in environmental conditions, such as from bright light to deep shade under a tree, or from an area that shows heavy trampling to an area with less.

B Decide which environmental factors you will measure and how you will measure them.

C Peg out the tape measure along the ground to form the transect line.

D Take measurements at regular intervals along the transect line (as shown in the diagram). Decide on your measurement intervals, which may depend on how long the line is and how much time you have to record information.

Practical Objective

To investigate the distribution of a species using a transect and quadrats.

Apparatus

- long tape measure (at least 20 m) with pegs at each end
- quadrat (e.g. 50 cm × 50 cm square)
- apparatus for measuring suitable abiotic factors, e.g. light sensor and recorder, soil humidity sensor, small bags for collecting soil samples for nutrient testing in the lab, trowel, anemometer (wind speed measurer)
- optional: identification charts, labels for bags and pencil

Safety

- Follow any safety guidance related to the working area.
- Consider the safety aspects of your chosen site, such as poisonous plants, animal faeces or open water, and take appropriate precautions while working.
- Wash your hands after the experiment.

E Place the top left-hand corner of the quadrat at a measurement point on the transect line.

F Measure the environmental factors at that point and record them. Collect any soil samples using a trowel and place them in a sealed bag. Label the bag clearly to identify its position along the transect.

G Record the abundance of your selected organisms in the quadrat.

H Repeat steps **F** and **G** at each measurement point along the transect.

I In the lab, carry out suitable tests on any soil samples and record the results.

# Edexcel GCSE (9–1)
Combined Science

CB9b Core practical 8: Quadrats and transects

Recording your results

1 In the space below, draw a table to record the abundance of the organisms you sampled at each point along the transect line, as well as the environmental factor measurements at each point.

2 Display your results in a suitable chart or graph.

Edexcel GCSE (9–1)
Combined Science

CB9b — Core practical 8: Quadrats and transects

Considering your results/conclusions

3 Describe the change in distribution of your chosen organism along the transect.

4 Describe the change in your chosen environmental factor along the transect.

5 Describe any correlation between the change in distribution of the organism and the change in environmental factor.

6 Suggest an explanation for any correlation that you have described in **5**.

Evaluation

7 Describe an experiment that you could do in the lab to test whether the environmental factor you measured affects the organism as you suggest in your answer to question **6**.

Edexcel GCSE (9–1)
Combined Science

CB9b Core practical 8: Quadrats and transects

Exam-style questions

1. Describe how a quadrat can be used to see if there is a relationship between the abundance of a plant and light intensity. (1)

2. What are abiotic factors? (1)

3. Name two abiotic factors, other than light intensity, that could change between the open ground and close to the tree, and explain why each factor could change. (2)

4. Explain why the abundance of a plant species might change between the open ground and close to the tree. (2)

5. Students used random quadrats to estimate the population of daisy plants on a field.
   a. Describe how the student could use these quadrats to estimate the number of daisy plants on the field. (3)

   b. The field had an area of 350 m². The students used 0.50 m² quadrats. The students found a mean of 0.21 daisy plants per quadrat.
   Estimate the population of daisy plants on the field. (2)

   Estimated population of daisy plants _____

Edexcel GCSE (9–1)
Combined Science

CC2d — Core practical 1: Investigating inks, Part 1

Part 1: Distillation procedure

Ink is a mixture of coloured substances dissolved in a liquid solvent. You will use simple distillation to separate a sample of the solvent in some ink. Read the method and answer the planning and predicting questions, before starting your experiment.

Your teacher may watch to see if you can:
- carry out experiments safely, reducing the risks from hazards.

Method

A Set up your apparatus as shown in the diagram. Put anti-bumping granules in the bottom of the flask.

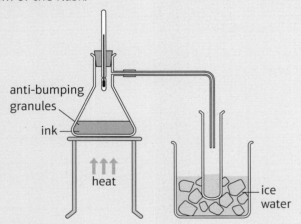

B Adjust the Bunsen burner so that you have a gentle blue flame. The air hole should be about half open and the gas tap should be about half on.

C Heat the ink until it boils.

D Collect the distillate in the test tube and note the temperature of the vapour.

Planning and predicting

1. When you distil the ink, how will you know if you have successfully purified the water?

2. Predict the temperature reading on the thermometer when the ink is boiling. Explain your answer.

3. What is the purpose of the ice water shown in the diagram?

Practical Objective

To use distillation to produce pure water from ink.

Apparatus

- eye protection
- conical flask with side arm
- delivery tube
- test tube
- ink
- Bunsen burner
- gauze
- rubber bung with thermometer
- 250 cm³ beaker
- ice
- tripod
- heat-resistant mat
- anti-bumping granules

Safety

- Eye protection should be worn at all times.
- Anti-bumping granules should be used to reduce the risk of the liquid boiling over.

Edexcel GCSE (9–1)
Combined Science

CC2d — Core practical 1: Investigating inks, Part 1

4 The conical flask might be knocked off the tripod.

  a Why is the conical flask a hazard if knocked over?

  b How can the risk of harm from this hazard be reduced?

5 Suggest one other hazard and a way of reducing the risk from this hazard.

6 What air hole and gas settings should you have for the Bunsen burner:

  a when you are not using it

  b when you are using it to heat the ink?

Considering your results/conclusions

7 Did you purify the water successfully? Explain your answer. Try to include a possible test you could carry out to show it was water.

8 Explain what happened when the ink was distilled. In your explanation, use the following words: boil, evaporate, liquid, steam, temperature, vapour.

Edexcel GCSE (9–1) Combined Science

CC2d — Core practical 1: Investigating inks, Part 1

Exam-style questions

1 A student carries out simple distillation on a sample of blue ink.

   a Predict how the appearance of the ink changes, and give a reason for your answer. (2)

   b During the experiment, the temperature around the bulb of the thermometer rises to 100 °C. Suggest an explanation for this. (1)

2 Explain why simple distillation allows a pure solvent to be separated from a solution. (3)

3 A student distils a sample of ink.
   Devise a simple method to show that the liquid collected is pure water.
   Include the expected results in your answer. (3)

Edexcel GCSE (9–1) Combined Science

CC2d — Core practical 1: Investigating inks, Part 2

Part 2: Chromatography procedure

Many inks contain a mixture of dyes. Chromatography can be used to identify inks; for example, inks from crime scenes or from documents that may have been forged.

Your teacher may watch to see if you can:
- follow instructions carefully
- draw conclusions from your results.

Practical Objective

You are going to test some inks to see how many dyes they contain and calculate their R_f values.

Apparatus
- pencil and ruler
- beaker
- chromatography paper attached to a pencil, rod or splint
- two marker pens or felt-tip pens

Method

A Check that your chromatography paper hangs close to the bottom of the empty beaker without touching it (as shown in the diagram).

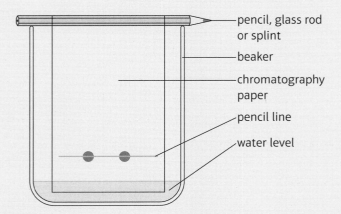

B Take the paper out of the beaker and draw a pencil line on the paper, about 2 cm from the bottom.

C Put a small spot of ink from each pen on your pencil line.

D Write the name of each pen or ink below each spot with a pencil.

E Pour some water into the beaker to a depth of about 1 cm.

F Lower the chromatography paper into the beaker so that the bottom of the paper is in the water, but the water level is below the spots (see the diagram).

G Leave the paper in the beaker until the water soaks up the paper and reaches near the top of the paper. The water is the solvent for the different coloured dye compounds in each ink. The solvent is called the mobile phase in chromatography, because it is the part that is moving.

H Take the paper out and immediately use a pencil to mark the location of the solvent front (the level the water has reached) before it evaporates. Leave the paper to dry.

Recording your results

1 Each ink is a mixture of several coloured dye compounds. Describe the coloured dye compounds that mix to produce the ink in each pen.

Edexcel GCSE (9–1)
Combined Science

CC2d Core practical 1: Investigating inks, Part 2

2 Measure the distance the solvent (the water) has risen from the pencil line.

3 Measure the distance that each dye spot has risen from the pencil line. Measure from the pencil line to the top of each different coloured spot.
Write your results in the tables below.

Name of pen/ink				
Colours of dye spots				
Distance of spot from pencil line (cm)				
R_f value				
Name of pen/ink				
Colours of dye spots				
Distance of spot from pencil line (cm)				
R_f value				

Considering your results/conclusions

4 Calculate the R_f value using the equation below for each separate colour in the inks.
Add this value to your table above.

$$R_f = \frac{\text{distance moved by the coloured spot}}{\text{distance moved by solvent}}$$

5 Were any of the inks a pure colour? Explain your conclusion.

6 Did the same coloured dyes appear in more than one ink?
If so, do you think they were the same chemical compound? Explain your answer.

Edexcel GCSE (9–1)
Combined Science

CC2d — Core practical 1: Investigating inks, Part 2

Evaluation

7 Why was the starting line drawn in pencil?

8 Why did you have to label the spots?

9 Why is the chromatography paper hung with the bottom just in the water?

10 Why must the water level in the beaker be below the spots?

11 How easy was it to identify the level to which each coloured dye had travelled? How would this affect the accuracy of the R_f values you calculated?

Edexcel GCSE (9–1)
Combined Science

CC2d Core practical 1: Investigating inks, Part 2

Exam-style questions

1 Propanone is a flammable solvent. A student carries out paper chromatography of ink using propanone.

   a Identify the mobile phase in her experiment. (1)

   b Identify the part of her apparatus that contained the stationary phase. (1)

   c Explain one precaution necessary to control the risk of harm in her experiment. (1)

   d Suggest an explanation for why the level of the propanone should be below the ink spot on the paper at the start. (1)

2 A student uses paper chromatography to analyse four samples of ink (X, A, B and C). The diagram shows his results.

   a Describe what the results tell you about ink sample X. (2)

   b Calculate the R_f value of the substance in ink B. (2)

Edexcel GCSE (9–1)
Combined Science

CC2d Core practical 1: Investigating inks, Part 2

3 A student carried out a paper chromatography test to identify the dyes in a sample of water-based ink. When she examined her chromatogram, she found that the solvent had travelled 9.15 cm and that one of the dyes had travelled 5.50 cm.
   Calculate the R_f value for this dye, giving your answer to 2 significant figures. Show your working. (3)

Edexcel GCSE (9–1)
Combined Science

CC8c Core practical 3: Preparing copper sulfate

Salts, such as copper sulfate, are compounds formed by reacting an acid with a base. Copper(II) oxide reacts with warm dilute sulfuric acid to produce a blue solution of the salt copper sulfate. In this practical, you will use these reactants to prepare pure, dry, hydrated copper sulfate crystals.

Practical Objective
To prepare a sample of pure, dry, hydrated copper sulfate crystals starting from copper(II) oxide.

Your teacher may watch to see if you can:
- safely and correctly use apparatus.

Apparatus
- eye protection
- 100 cm³ conical flask
- 100 cm³ beaker
- Bunsen burner
- gauze and tripod
- heat mat
- Petri dish or watch glass
- 100 cm³ measuring cylinder
- evaporating basin
- spatula
- stirring rod
- clamp, stand and boss
- filter funnel
- filter paper
- tongs
- water bath (set at 50 °C)
- dilute sulfuric acid
- copper(II) oxide

Method

A Pour about 20 cm³ of dilute sulfuric acid into a conical flask.

B Place the conical flask into a water bath at 50 °C and heat for 3–4 minutes to allow the acid to heat up.

C Use the spatula to add a little copper(II) oxide to the acid and stir or swirl the contents of the flask.

D Keep repeating step C until the black powder does not disappear after stirring. (This makes sure the copper(II) oxide is in excess.)

E Return the mixture to the water bath for a few minutes (to make sure there is no acid left).

F Filter the mixture into a beaker and pour into an evaporating basin.

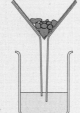
Step F

G Place the evaporating basin on top of a beaker half full of water. Heat the beaker, evaporating basin and contents using a Bunsen burner on a blue flame.

H Heat until about half of the water has evaporated. Then allow the evaporating basin to cool.

I When cool, transfer the solution to a Petri dish or watch glass and leave for a few days to allow the water to evaporate.

J Observe the shape and colour of the copper sulfate crystals formed.

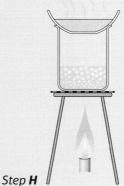
Step H

Safety
- Wear eye protection at all times.

Recording your results

1 Describe the colour, shape and size of the copper sulfate crystals produced.

2 Describe the appearance of:
   a the sulfuric acid

   b the copper(II) oxide

   c the solution at the end of the reaction.

Edexcel GCSE (9–1)
Combined Science

CC8c Core practical 3: Preparing copper sulfate

Considering your results

3   Write a word equation to show the reaction you have carried out.

4   State why you need to be sure excess copper(II) oxide is added in step **D**.

5   What would happen in step **E** if there was still some acid left?

6   Name the substance left in the filter paper in step **F**.

7   What is dissolved in the solution that went through the filter paper?

8   Explain why this is an example of a neutralisation reaction.

9   What substance acts as a base in this reaction?

10 Write a symbol equation to show the reaction you have carried out. Include the state symbols. Use your answer to question **3** to help you.

Edexcel GCSE (9–1)
Combined Science

CC8c Core practical 3: Preparing copper sulfate

Exam-style questions

1. State why copper sulfate is described as a salt. (1)

2. During the preparation of copper sulfate the mixture is filtered to remove copper(II) oxide.
   Explain why the copper(II) oxide gets stuck in the filter paper while the copper sulfate goes through it. (2)

3. Nickel chloride ($NiCl_2$) is a soluble salt.
   It can be made by reacting insoluble nickel oxide (NiO) with hydrochloric acid (HCl).

   a. Write a word equation for this reaction. (1)

   b. Write a balanced equation with state symbols. (2)

4. You are given a sample of copper sulfate solution.
   Devise a procedure to obtain a pure, dry sample of hydrated copper sulfate crystals.
   Include details of the apparatus you will need.
   You may draw diagrams to help with your answer. (4)

Edexcel GCSE (9–1)
Combined Science

CC8c Core practical 3: Preparing copper sulfate

5 Two class groups prepared some zinc chloride. One group produced lots of very small crystals while the other group produced larger crystals. Suggest an explanation for the groups producing different-sized crystals.

(2)

Edexcel GCSE (9–1)
Combined Science

CC8d — Core practical 2: Investigating neutralisation

Stomach acid contains hydrochloric acid. Acid indigestion causes a burning feeling in the chest and throat. Antacids, which may contain magnesium hydroxide, are used to neutralise stomach acid to relieve indigestion.
In this practical, you will use calcium hydroxide, which has similar properties to magnesium hydroxide, to investigate neutralisation.

Your teacher may watch to see if you can:
- carry out an experiment appropriately
- use apparatus accurately and safely.

Method

A Use the measuring cylinder to add $50\,cm^3$ of dilute hydrochloric acid to the beaker.

B Estimate and record the pH of the contents of the beaker, as follows:
- Put a piece of universal indicator paper onto the white tile.
- Dip the end of the glass rod into the liquid, then tap it onto the universal indicator paper.
- Wait 30 seconds, then match the colour to the appropriate pH on the pH colour chart.
- Rinse the glass rod with water.

C Measure out $0.3\,g$ of calcium hydroxide powder onto a piece of paper or a 'weighing boat'.

D Add the calcium hydroxide powder to the beaker, stir, then estimate and record the pH of the mixture (as in step **B**).

E Repeat step **D** seven times so that you add a total of $2.4\,g$ of calcium hydroxide powder to the acid.

Recording your results

1. In the space below, make a table to record the pH of the contents of the beaker. Use columns for the mass of calcium hydroxide powder added, and the pH of the mixture. Remember to leave a row for the first pH measurement (before you have added any calcium hydroxide).

Practical Objective

Powdered calcium hydroxide reacts with hydrochloric acid. Calcium chloride solution and water are produced:

$$Ca(OH)_2(s) + 2HCl(aq) \rightarrow CaCl_2(aq) + 2H_2O(l)$$

You will investigate what happens to the pH of a fixed volume of dilute hydrochloric acid when you add calcium hydroxide to it.

Apparatus

- eye protection
- $100\,cm^3$ beaker
- $50\,cm^3$ measuring cylinder
- $\pm 0.1\,g$ balance
- piece of paper or a 'weighing boat'
- spatula
- stirring rod
- white tile
- universal indicator paper
- pH colour chart
- dilute hydrochloric acid
- calcium hydroxide powder
- graph paper

Safety

- Wear eye protection. Calcium hydroxide is an irritant with a risk of serious damage to eyes. Dilute hydrochloric acid is an irritant.

Edexcel GCSE (9–1)
Combined Science

CC8d — Core practical 2: Investigating neutralisation

Considering your results

2   Plot a line graph to show pH on the vertical axis and mass of calcium hydroxide added on the horizontal axis. Draw a curve of best fit.

3   Describe what happens to the pH of the reaction mixture as calcium hydroxide continues to be added.

4   Use your graph to determine the mass of calcium hydroxide that must be added to reach pH 7.

Evaluation

5   Explain one way to improve the accuracy of the experiment.

Edexcel GCSE (9–1)
Combined Science

CC8d Core practical 2: Investigating neutralisation

Exam-style questions

1. **a** Name the soluble salt formed when hydrochloric acid reacts with calcium hydroxide. (1)

   b Write the balanced equation, including state symbols, for the reaction between calcium hydroxide powder and dilute hydrochloric acid. (3)

2. Give **two** reasons that explain why eye protection must be worn when using dilute hydrochloric acid. (2)

3. A student investigates the change in pH when calcium hydroxide powder is added to 100 cm³ of dilute hydrochloric acid.

   a State **two** control variables in this experiment. (2)

   b State the independent variable in this experiment. (1)

   c Describe how the student could modify the experiment to investigate temperature changes instead of pH changes. (1)

Edexcel GCSE (9–1)
Combined Science

CC8d Core practical 2: Investigating neutralisation

4 The pH of a solution may be determined using universal indicator paper or using a pH meter.

   a State why a pH meter must be calibrated using a solution with a known pH value. (1)

   b Explain whether indicator paper or a pH meter has the higher resolution. (2)

Edexcel GCSE (9–1)
Combined Science

CC10a — Core practical 4: Electrolysis of copper sulfate solution

The copper produced for making copper wires must be very pure. It is produced by electrolysis of copper sulfate solution.

Your teacher may watch to see if you can:
- carefully control variables during investigations
- make accurate measurements.

Method 1 – Using copper electrodes

A   Select two pieces of copper foil to use as electrodes and clean them with emery paper. Label one of the electrodes as 'anode' and the other as 'cathode'.

B   Measure and record the mass of each electrode.

C   Half fill the beaker with copper sulfate solution.

D   Set up the circuit as shown in the diagram.

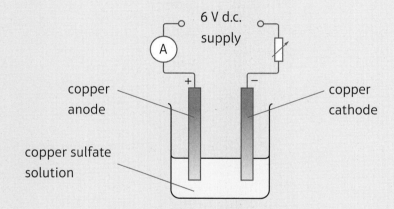

E   Turn the power on and adjust the variable resistor to give a current of 0.2 A. Record the current. Leave the power on for 20 minutes, adjusting the variable resistor to keep the current constant, if necessary.

F   Then turn off the power and remove the electrodes from the beaker.

G   Gently rinse the electrodes with distilled water and then dip them into propanone. Remove the electrodes from the propanone and gently shake them until the propanone evaporates.

H   Measure and record the masses of the dry electrodes.

I   Repeat the experiment using currents of 0.3 A, 0.4 A and 0.5 A.

Practical Objective
To electrolyse copper sulfate solution using inert (graphite) electrodes and copper electrodes.

Apparatus
- eye protection
- emery paper
- low voltage d.c. supply
- ammeter
- variable resistor
- connecting leads
- crocodile clips
- 100 cm³ beaker
- stop clock
- two graphite rods
- two pieces of copper foil
- copper sulfate solution
- distilled water
- access to propanone (in a fume cupboard)
- access to a balance

Safety
- Wear eye protection.
- Propanone is an irritant. It is highly flammable; there must not be any naked flames in the laboratory.

Recording your results

1   Record your results in the table below, including the change in mass of each electrode.

Current (A)	Mass of anode at start (g)	Mass of anode at end (g)	Change in mass of anode (g)	Mass of cathode at start (g)	Mass of cathode at end (g)	Change in mass of cathode (g)

Considering your results/conclusions

2 Plot a graph of change in mass of the anode against the current. Draw a line of best fit through the points. Plot a second graph on the same axes showing the change in mass of the cathode against the current. Again, draw a line of best fit through these points.

3 Describe the relationship between the change in mass at each electrode and the current.

4 Explain the changes in mass of each electrode.

5 Use the diagram to predict the change in mass of the anode when the current is 0.35 A.

6 Suggest a reason why the change in mass at the cathode is not the same as the change in mass at the anode when the same current is used.

7 Describe how you could improve the experiment to be more certain that the data collected is correct and free from error.

Edexcel GCSE (9–1) Combined Science

CC10a — Core practical 4: Electrolysis of copper sulfate solution

Method 2 – Using inert electrodes

A The diagram on the right shows the circuit used for the electrolysis of copper sulfate solution with graphite electrodes. Set up the circuit as shown.

B Turn the power on.

C Observe what happens at each electrode.

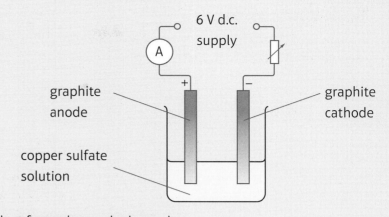

Recording your results

1 Record your observations and the name of the product formed at each electrode.

Considering your results/conclusions

2 Explain the formation of the product at each electrode.

H 3 Write a half equation for the formation of the product at each electrode and classify each reaction as oxidation or reduction.

Edexcel GCSE (9–1) Combined Science

CC10a Core practical 4: Electrolysis of copper sulfate solution

Exam-style questions

1. Explain why a different product is formed at the anode when copper sulfate solution is electrolysed using graphite electrodes rather than copper electrodes. (4)

2. Look at the method for electrolysis using copper electrodes.

    a State and explain one safety precaution. (1)

    b State why it is important to use clean copper electrodes. (1)

    c Give a reason why a variable resistor is used in the electrolysis circuit. (1)

    d Suggest a reason why the electrodes are washed at the end of the electrolysis. (1)

    e Suggest a reason why propanone is used after washing the electrodes with distilled water. (1)

Edexcel GCSE (9–1) Combined Science — CC14a & b

Core practical 6: Investigating reaction rates, Part 1

Part 1: Measuring the production of a gas

The progress of a chemical reaction can be measured by how the amounts of reactant or product change with time.

Your teacher may watch to see if you can:
- carefully control variables during investigations
- measure change accurately.

Method

Task 1

A. Set up the apparatus as shown in the diagram.

B. Measure 40 cm³ of 1 mol dm⁻³ (36.5 g dm⁻³) hydrochloric acid into a conical flask.

C. Add 5 g of small marble chips to the flask.

D. Immediately stopper the flask and start the stop clock/watch.

E. Note the total volume of gas produced after every 30 seconds for five minutes or until the reaction has finished.

F. Repeat steps **A** to **E** using 5 g of larger marble chips.

Task 2

G. Follow steps **A** to **D** above.

H. Note the amount of carbon dioxide produced in one minute.

I. Repeat steps **G** and **H** using 0.8 mol dm⁻³ (29.2 g dm⁻³), 0.6 mol dm⁻³ (21.9 g dm⁻³), 0.4 mol dm⁻³ (14.6 g dm⁻³) and 0.2 mol dm⁻³ (7.3 g dm⁻³) acid.

Practical Objective
To investigate the effect on the rate of reaction of changing the surface area of solids and the concentration of solutions, by measuring the production of a gas.

Apparatus
- eye protection
- balance
- water trough or beehive shelf
- 100 cm³ measuring cylinder
- stop clock
- conical flask
- delivery tube and bung
- marble chips (small)
- marble chips (large)
- dilute hydrochloric acid (1 mol dm⁻³ or 36.5 g dm⁻³)

Safety
- Wear eye protection at all times.
- Care is needed with acid solutions. Wash off splashes immediately.

Recording your results

Task 1
Record your results in the table below.

Time (min)	0	0.5	1.0	1.5	2.0	2.5	3.0	3.5	4.0	4.5	5.0
Small chips – volume of gas (cm³)											
Large chips – volume of gas (cm³)											

Task 2
Record your results in the table below.

Concentration of acid (mol dm⁻³)	1.0	0.8	0.6	0.4	0.2
Volume of gas produced in one minute (cm³)					

Edexcel GCSE (9–1) Combined Science — CC14a & b

Core practical 6: Investigating reaction rates, Part 1

Considering your results/conclusion

Task 1

1. Use your results to draw a graph of volume of gas against time for small chips and a graph for large chips on the same axes. Put time on the horizontal axis and volume of gas on the vertical axis. Draw a line of best fit for each graph using different coloured lines and labels.

2. Explain how you can tell from the graphs when the reactions were finished.

3. Describe how the size of the marble chips is related to the surface area for a fixed mass of chips.

4. Describe how increasing the surface area affects the rate of reaction.

Edexcel GCSE (9–1) Combined Science
CC14a & b — Core practical 6: Investigating reaction rates, Part 1

5 Explain how your results and graphs fit with your conclusion in question **4**.

Task 2

6 Use your results to draw a graph of concentration of acid against volume of gas produced in one minute. Put volume of gas on the horizontal axis and concentration on the vertical axis.

7 Describe how the rate of the reaction is related to the concentration of the acid.

8 Explain how your results and diagram fit with your conclusion in question **7**.

Evaluation

Tasks 1 & 2

9 Suggest possible sources of error in these investigations.

10 Suggest possible changes to the methods of both tasks that could improve the reliability of the results.

Exam-style question

1. Devise a plan to investigate the effect of changing concentration of acid on the rate of reaction between sulfuric acid (H_2SO_4) and magnesium carbonate ($MgCO_3$).
Your plan should include details of the equipment you will need, the measurements you will take and record, the variables which you will need to control, and any safety precautions you should take.

(6)

Edexcel GCSE (9–1) Combined Science — CC14a & b

Core practical 6: Investigating reaction rates, Part 2

Part 2: Observing a colour change

The progress of a chemical reaction can be measured by how long a reaction takes to reach a certain point.

Your teacher may watch to see if you can:
- carefully control variables during investigations
- measure change accurately
- work safely.

Method

A Decide on four temperatures between 20 °C and 50 °C, which you are going to investigate.

B Place 10 cm³ of sodium thiosulfate solution and 40 cm³ of water into a 250 cm³ conical flask.

C Measure 5 cm³ of dilute hydrochloric acid into a test tube.

D Clamp the conical flask in place in a water bath at your first chosen temperature. Place the test tube in a rack in the same water bath.

E Record your chosen temperature.

F After five minutes, remove the flask and place it on a piece of white paper marked with a cross, as shown opposite.

G Add the acid to the thiosulfate solution, quickly cover the top of the flask with cling film and start the stop clock.

H Looking down from above, stop the clock when the cross disappears.

I Note this time and the final temperature of the mixture.

J Repeat steps **A** to **I** for the other chosen temperatures.

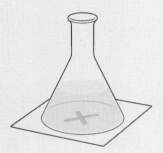

Practical Objective

To investigate the effect of changing the temperature on the rate of reaction between sodium thiosulfate and hydrochloric acid, by observing a colour change in the solutions.

Apparatus
- eye protection
- 250 cm³ conical flask
- 10 cm³ measuring cylinder
- 50 cm³ measuring cylinder
- stop clock
- test tube
- test tube rack
- water bath
- white paper with cross
- sodium thiosulfate solution
- dilute hydrochloric acid
- cling film

Safety
- Wear eye protection at all times.
- Care is needed with acid solutions. Wash off splashes immediately.
- Do not exceed 50 °C

Recording your results

1 Draw a table in the space below with two columns: one for temperature, and the other for the time taken for the cross to disappear. Don't forget the units. Record the results of your experiments.

Edexcel GCSE (9–1) Combined Science — CC14a & b
Core practical 6: Investigating reaction rates, Part 2

Considering your results/conclusion

2 Draw a graph of your results, with temperature on the horizontal axis. Draw a line of best fit.

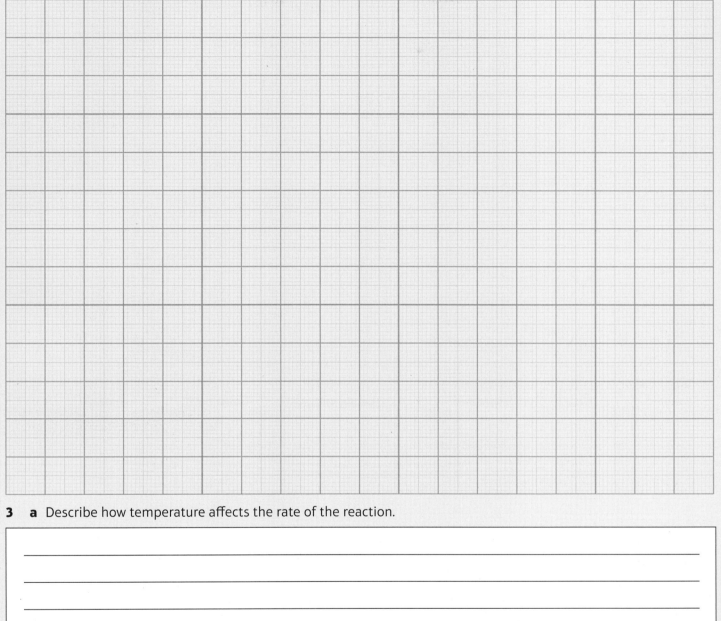

3 **a** Describe how temperature affects the rate of the reaction.

b Explain your answer to part **a** by referring to the shape of your diagram.

Edexcel GCSE (9–1) Combined Science
CC14a & b — Core practical 6: Investigating reaction rates, Part 2

4 If the rate of reaction doubled, what would happen to the time taken for the cross to disappear?

5 a What temperature rise roughly doubles the rate of the reaction?

b Use the values from your graph to explain your answer to part **a**.

Evaluation

6 Describe two possible sources of error in this investigation.

7 Suggest a way of reducing one of these errors.

Edexcel GCSE (9–1) Combined Science
CC14a & b — Core practical 6: Investigating reaction rates, Part 2

Exam-style questions

1 Explain why acid reacts faster with powdered chalk than with lumps of chalk. (3)

2 Some results from a 'disappearing cross' experiment are shown in the table.

Mean temperature (°C)	Time taken for cross to disappear (s)
20	165
30	81
40	42
50	21

   a State why the cross disappears. (1)

   b Sketch a graph of the results with temperature on the horizontal axis. (3)

   c Explain what these results tell you about the effect of temperature on the rate of this reaction. (2)

   d Describe one way of improving the results obtained from this investigation. (1)

Edexcel GCSE (9–1)
Combined Science

CP2d Core practical 1: Investigating acceleration

In drag racing, the aim is to get to the end of a straight track as quickly as possible. The most important feature of the bike is its acceleration. Drag racers try to improve the performance of their bikes by changing the force produced by the engine and the tyres or by changing the mass of the bike. In this practical, you are going to use trolleys as a model of a motorbike to investigate the effects that mass and force have on acceleration.

Your teacher may watch to see if you can:
- follow instructions safely
- take careful measurements.

Method

A Prop up one end of the ramp and place a trolley on it. Adjust the slope of the ramp until the trolley just starts to move on its own. Gravity pulling the trolley down the slope is now slightly greater than the friction in the trolley's wheels.

B Stick a piece of card to the top of the trolley using sticky putty. Leave enough space to stack some masses on top of the trolley. Measure the length of the card and write it down.

C Find the mass of the trolley and write it down.

D Fasten the pulley at the bottom end of the ramp, and arrange the string and masses as shown below.

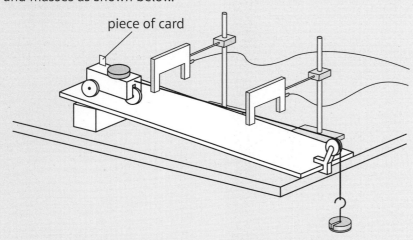

E Set up two light gates, one near the top of the ramp and one near the bottom.
Adjust their positions so that the card on the top of the trolley passes through each gate as it runs down the ramp.

F Put a mass on the end of the string. You will keep this mass the same for all your tests. You will have to decide what mass to use.

G Release the trolley from the top of the ramp and write down the speed of the trolley (from the datalogger) as it passes through *each* light gate. Also write down the time it takes for the trolley to go from one light gate to the other.

H Repeat step **G** for other masses on the trolley. You will have to decide what masses to use, how many different masses you are going to test, and whether you need to repeat any of your tests.

Practical Objective
To investigate the effect of mass on the acceleration of a trolley.

Apparatus
- trolley
- ramp
- blocks to prop up the end of the ramp
- string
- pulley
- masses
- sticky tape
- card
- sticky putty
- balance
- two light gates
- datalogger
- two clamps and stands
- box of crumpled newspaper

Safety
- Make sure masses cannot fall on your feet by placing a box of crumpled newspaper on the floor beneath them.

Edexcel GCSE (9–1)
Combined Science

CP2d — Core practical 1: Investigating acceleration

Prediction

1. You will accelerate a trolley using a constant force. What effect do you think the mass of the trolley will have on the acceleration? Explain your prediction if you can. Record your prediction and ideas in the box below.

Recording your results

2. Record your results in the table below.

Mass added to trolley (kg)	Total mass of trolley and masses (kg)	Run number	u – 1st velocity reading (m/s)	v – 2nd velocity reading (m/s)	Time between velocity measurements (s)	Acceleration (m/s²)
		1				
		2				
		3				
		Mean				

3. Calculate the acceleration for each run using the equation in the box.
4. Find the mean acceleration for each trolley mass.

> You will need to recall and apply this equation in the exam.
>
> $$\text{acceleration} = \frac{\text{change in velocity}}{\text{time}}$$
>
> $$a = \frac{(v - u)}{t}$$

Considering your results

5. Plot a graph to show your results. Put the total mass of the trolley on the horizontal axis and the acceleration on the vertical axis, as shown in the diagram. Draw a line or curve of best fit through your points, and identify any of your results that are anomalous.

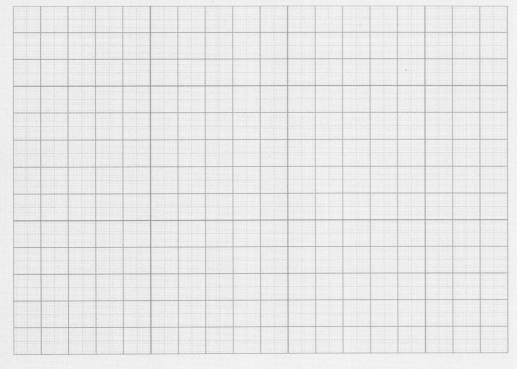

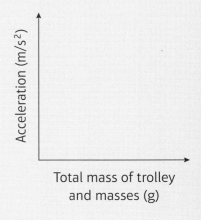

Edexcel GCSE (9–1)
Combined Science

CP2d Core practical 1: Investigating acceleration

6 a What relationship between acceleration and mass does your graph show?

b Is this what you predicted?

Evaluation

7 a How close are the points on your graph to the line of best fit? Comment on any of your results that are anomalous.

b What does this tell you about the quality of the data you have gathered?

8 How do your results compare to the results obtained by other groups?

9 How certain are you that your conclusion is correct? Explain your answer.

Edexcel GCSE (9–1)
Combined Science
CP2d — Core practical 1: Investigating acceleration

Exam-style questions

1. The light gates and datalogger record the speed of the trolley at the top of the ramp and at the bottom of the ramp, and also record the time the trolley takes to move between the two light gates. Describe how this information can be used to calculate the acceleration. (2)

2. Use the results shown in this graph to draw a conclusion. (1)

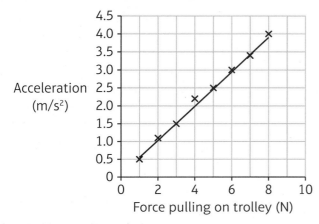

3. Look at this graph.

Use this graph to draw a conclusion. (1)

4. Use the graph in question **2** to calculate the mass of the trolley used in the investigation. (3)

mass = _____ kg

Combined Science

Edexcel GCSE (9–1)

CP4b — Core practical 2: Investigating waves, Part 1

The speed, frequency and wavelength of waves can be measured in different ways. The most suitable equipment for carrying out these measurements depends on the type of wave and on its speed.

Your teacher may watch to see if you can:
- follow instructions carefully
- make accurate measurements.

Part 1: Speed of waves on water

Method

A Set up a ripple tank with a straight dipper near one of the short sides of the tank. Fasten a ruler to one of the long sides so you can see the markings above the water level.

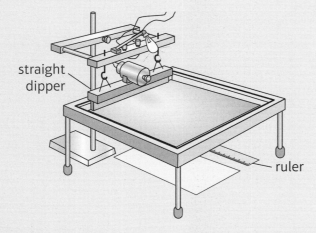

B Vary the current to the motor until you get waves with a wavelength about half as long as the ripple tank (so you can always see two waves).

C Count how many waves are formed in 10 seconds and write it down in the space below.

D Look at the waves against the ruler. Use the markings on the ruler to estimate the wavelength of the waves. If you have one, use a camera to take a photo of the waves with a ruler held just above them. Write your estimated wavelength down in the space below.

E Mark two points on the edge of the ripple tank and measure the distance between them. Use the stop clock to find out how long it takes a wave to go from one mark to the other. Add this value in the space below.

Practical Objective
To measure waves in different ways and evaluate the suitability of the equipment.

Apparatus
- ripple tank
- stop clock
- ruler
- digital camera

Safety
- Mop up any spilled water straight away.

Recording your results

Number of waves counted [step **C**]:

Estimated wavelength [step **D**]:

Distance between two points [step **E**]:

Time taken for wave to go between two points [step **E**]:

Edexcel GCSE (9–1) Combined Science

CP4b — Core practical 2: Investigating waves, Part 1

Using your results

1. Calculate the speed of a single wave by dividing the distance by the time (both from step **E**). Make sure your distance is in metres and your time is in seconds.

2. Find the frequency by taking the number of waves in 10 seconds (from step **C**) and dividing by 10. Then calculate the speed of the series of waves by using the equation:

   wave speed = frequency × wavelength

   You will need to recall and apply this equation in the exam.

Considering your results/conclusions

3. Compare your results from questions **1** and **2** with results obtained by other groups. Are your results similar? If not, can you explain the differences?

Evaluation

4. How easy was it to measure the frequency in step **C**? Why did you count the number of waves in 10 seconds?

5. How easy was it to measure the wavelength in step **D**? It was suggested that you use a camera to help you do this. What benefit would there be in doing this?

6. How easy was it to time a single wave in step **E**? Is there any way you could improve this measurement?

Combined Science

Edexcel GCSE (9–1)

CP4b — Core practical 2: Investigating waves, Part 2

Part 2: Measuring waves in a solid

Method

A Suspend a metal rod horizontally using clamp stands and rubber bands, as shown in the diagram below.

B Hit one end of the rod with a hammer. Hold a smartphone with a frequency app near the rod and note down the peak frequency.

C Measure the length of the rod and write it down. The wavelength will be twice the length of the rod.

Apparatus

- metre rule
- hammer
- two clamps and stands
- long metal rod
- rubber bands
- smartphone with frequency app

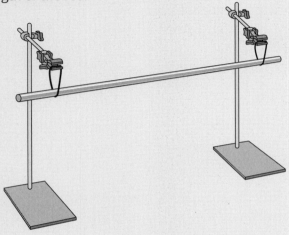

Recording your results

1. Use the frequency (from step **B**) and the wavelength (from step **C**) to calculate the speed of sound in the metal rod.

Frequency [step **B**]: _____

Wavelength [step **C**]: _____

Your calculation for the speed of sound in the metal rod:

Considering your results/conclusions

2. What is the speed of sound in the material you tested?

Edexcel GCSE (9–1)
Combined Science

CP4b Core practical 2: Investigating waves, Part 2

Evaluation

3 Explain which of your measurements is the more accurate: the wavelength or the frequency.

4 Complete the table to summarise the equipment you used for the measurements in both parts of this investigation, and how suitable the equipment was.

What was measured?	Which material was this measured for?	How was it measured?	Why was this method chosen?

5 You can measure walking speed using a tape measure and a stop clock. Explain why these instruments are not suitable for measuring the speed of sound in a solid.

Edexcel GCSE (9–1)
Combined Science

CP4b — Core practical 2: Investigating waves

Exam-style questions

1. **a** State the equation relating the speed of sound, frequency and wavelength. (1)

   b A sound wave in air travels 660 metres in 2 seconds. Calculate the speed of the sound wave. Recall and state the equation used. (2)

   _____ m/s

2. A sound wave travelling in water has a frequency of 100 Hz. The speed of sound in water is 1482 m/s. Calculate the wavelength of the wave. Give your answer to 2 significant figures. (2)

   _____ m

3. Adanna is watching waves on the sea go past two buoys. She knows the buoys are 20 metres apart. Describe how she can find the speed of the waves. (2)

Edexcel GCSE (9–1)
Combined Science

CP4b Core practical 2: Investigating waves

4 a The speed of sound can be measured in the laboratory using an electronic timer and two microphones. Describe how you would measure the speed of sound using this equipment.
You may draw a labelled diagram if it helps your answer. (4)

b Explain why an electronic timer was used and not a stop clock. (2)

Edexcel GCSE (9-1)
Combined Science

CP5a — Core practical 3: Investigating refraction

Electromagnetic waves travel at different speeds in different materials. Light slows down when it goes from air into glass or water. If light hits the interface at an angle, it changes direction. This is called refraction. In this practical, you will investigate how the direction of a ray of light changes as it enters and leaves a glass block.

Your teacher may watch to see if you can:
- measure angles accurately.

Method

A Place a piece of plain paper on the desk. Set up the power supply, ray box and single slit so that you can shine a single ray of light across the paper on your desk.

B Place a rectangular glass block on the paper. Draw around the block.

C Shine a ray of light into your block. Use small crosses to mark where the rays of light go.

Join the points where the light enters and leaves the glass block, and draw a normal.

D Take the block off the paper. Use a ruler to join the crosses and show the path of the light, and extend the line so it meets the outline of the block. Join the points where the light entered and left the block to show where it travelled inside the block.

E Measure the angles of incidence and refraction where the light entered the block, and measure the angles where it left the block.

F Repeat steps **C** to **E** with the ray entering the block at different angles.

G Move the ray box so that the light ray reaches the interface at right angles. Note what happens to the light as it enters and leaves the block.

Practical Objective
To investigate how light is affected when it travels from air into glass, or from glass into air.

Apparatus
- ray box with single slit
- power supply
- rectangular glass block
- ruler
- protractor
- plain paper

Safety
- Ray boxes may get hot.

Recording your results

1 Record your results in this table.

Air to glass (light entering the block)		Glass to air (light leaving the block)	
Angle i	Angle r	Angle i	Angle r

2 Draw a graph to show your results. Put the angle of incidence on the horizontal axis. Plot the air-to-glass points and draw a smooth curve of best fit. Repeat for the glass-to-air points, on the same set of axes.

Considering your results

3 Describe the results shown by your diagram.

4 How does the direction of the ray of light leaving the glass block compare with the direction of the ray entering it?

5 Write a conclusion for your investigation.

Evaluation

6 a How accurate were your measurements?

   b Is there any way you could improve your measurements?

Edexcel GCSE (9–1)
Combined Science

CP5a — Core practical 3: Investigating refraction

Exam-style questions

1. Describe the difference between the way that light travels through glass compared with the way in which it travels through air. (1)

2. The table shows a student's results from this investigation.

Air to glass		Glass to air	
i	r	i	r
10°	6°	6°	6°
20°	13°	13°	20°
30°	20°	20°	31°
40°	25°	25°	40°
50°	45°	30°	50°
60°	34°	34°	58°
70°	38°	38°	69°
80°	40°	40°	78°

a Use the data in the table to plot a graph to show the results for light going from air to glass. Put the angle of incidence on the horizontal axis, and join your points with a smooth curve of best fit, identifying any anomalous results. (5)

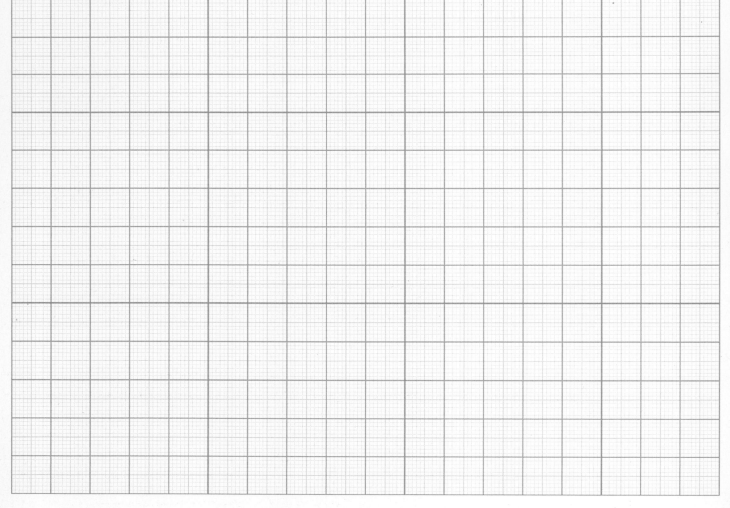

72

b Use the table and your diagram to write a conclusion for this part of the investigation. (3)

c Use your graph to find the angle of refraction when the angle of incidence is 15°. (1)

3 If light passes through a glass block with parallel sides, the ray that comes out should be parallel with the ray that goes in. This means that the angle of incidence for air to glass should be the same as the angle of refraction from glass to air.

Look at the table in question **2**. Suggest one source of random error that may have caused the differences in these angles. (1)

Edexcel GCSE (9–1)
Combined Science

CP9e — Core practical 5: Investigating resistance

Engineers who design circuits need to know the characteristics of different circuit components. Resistors are used to control the flow of current in a circuit but not all components keep the same resistance if the potential difference across them changes.

Your teacher may watch to see if you can:
- follow instructions to work safely
- make accurate measurements.

Task 1 – Investigating resistance
Method

A Connect circuit X as shown in the diagram.

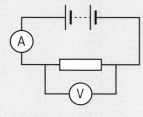

Circuit X

B Set the power pack to a potential difference of 1 V and switch it on. Record the readings on the ammeter and voltmeter in a table and then switch off the power.

C Repeat step **B** for settings on the power pack of 2 V, 3 V, 4 V, 5 V and 6 V.

D Replace the resistor in circuit X with a filament lamp. Repeat steps **B** and **C**.

Recording your results

1 Record your results for circuit X in the table below.

Potential difference (V)	Current (A)	
	Resistor	Filament lamp
0	0	0
1		
2		
3		
4		
5		
6		

Practical Objective
To investigate the relationship between potential difference, current and resistance for a resistor and a filament lamp.

Apparatus
- power supply
- ammeter
- connecting wires
- two crocodile clips
- voltmeter
- resistor
- two filament lamps

Safety
- Never use mains electricity for practical work with circuits.
- Ask your teacher to check your circuit before you switch it on.

Edexcel GCSE (9–1)
Combined Science

CP9e Core practical 5: Investigating resistance

Considering your results/conclusions

2   Plot a graph of your results. Plot the independent variable (potential difference) on the horizontal axis and the dependent variable (current) on the vertical axis. Use the same axes for both the resistor and the filament lamp. Draw two lines or curves of best fit, one through each set of points. Make sure you label the lines, and identify any anomalous results.

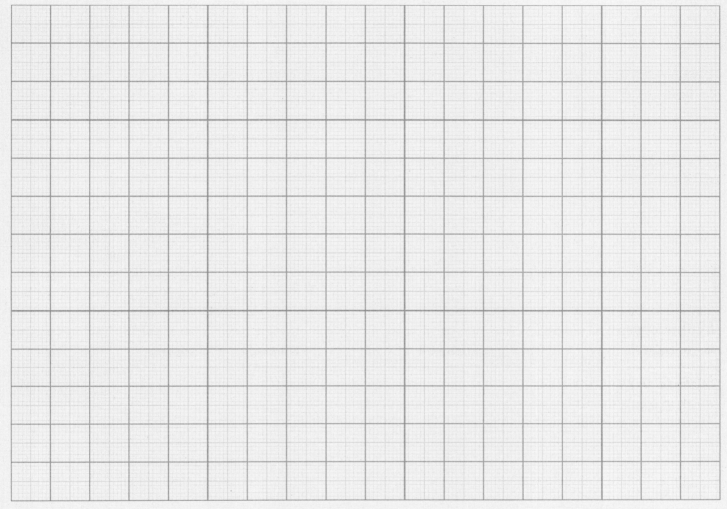

You can calculate the resistance from the potential difference and the current, using the equation on the right. You will need to learn this for the exam.

$$\text{resistance } (\Omega) = \frac{\text{potential difference (V)}}{\text{current (A)}}$$

3   **a**   Calculate the resistance of the resistor when the potential difference is 1 V and when it is 6 V.

b Calculate the resistance of the filament lamp when the potential difference is 1 V and when it is 6 V.

c Draw a conclusion about how the resistance of the two components changes with increasing potential difference.

d Use evidence from your graph and your calculations to explain how you came to your conclusion.

Evaluation

4 a Looking at your graph for the resistor, how close were your points to the line of best fit?

b What does this tell you about the quality of data you have gathered?

5 How reproducible were your results? (Compare your results with other groups.)

Edexcel GCSE (9–1)
Combined Science

CP9e Core practical 5: Investigating resistance

Task 2 – Filament lamps in series and parallel circuits

Prediction

6. Look at circuits Y and Z below. Explain how you think the readings will compare in the two circuits for:

   a the ammeters   b the voltmeters.

   _____
   _____
   _____

Practical Objective

To test series and parallel circuits using resistors and filament lamps.

Apparatus

- power supply
- three voltmeters
- three ammeters
- connecting wires
- two crocodile clips
- two filament lamps

Method

A Connect the circuit shown in circuit Y.

B Set the power pack to 1 V and switch it on. Record the readings on the ammeter and the voltmeters, and then switch off the power.

C Repeat step **B** for settings on the power pack of 2 V, 3 V, 4 V, 5 V and 6 V.

D Now set up the circuit shown in circuit Z.

E Set the power pack to 1 V and switch it on. Record the readings on the ammeters and the voltmeters, and then switch off the power.

F Repeat step **E** for settings on the power pack of 2 V, 3 V, 4 V, 5 V and 6 V.

Safety

- Never use mains electricity for practical work with circuits.
- Ask your teacher to check your circuit before you switch it on.

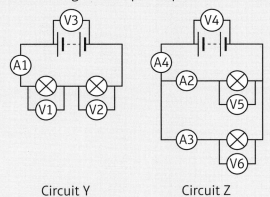

Circuit Y   Circuit Z

Recording your results

7. Record your results for circuits Y and Z in the table below.

Potential difference (volts)	Circuit Y (lamps in series)				Circuit Z (lamps in parallel)					
	A1	V1	V2	V3	A2	A3	A4	V4	V5	V6
0	0	0	0	0	0	0	0	0	0	0
1										
2										
3										
4										
5										
6										

Edexcel GCSE (9–1)
Combined Science

CP9e Core practical 5: Investigating resistance

Considering your results/conclusions

8 a Compare the total current in the circuit through the two filament lamps when they are connected in series and when they are connected in parallel.

b Compare the potential difference across the two filament lamps when they are connected in series and in parallel.

9 How does changing the potential difference across each circuit affect how these values compare?

Evaluation

10 Suggest what the answer would be to question **9** if fixed resistors replaced the lamps in the two circuits.

Edexcel GCSE (9–1) Combined Science

CP9e Core practical 5: Investigating resistance

Exam-style questions

1. State the units for measuring resistance. (1)

2. Tables 1 and 2 show some results from the investigation on filament lamps in series and parallel circuits (shown in circuits A and B).

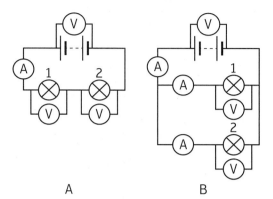

A   B

Table 1

	Potential difference (V)		
	Power pack	Lamp 1	Lamp 2
Series (A)	4	2	2
Parallel (B)	4	4	4

Table 2

	Current (A)		
	Power pack	Lamp 1	Lamp 2
Series (A)	0.23	(x)	(y)
Parallel (B)	(z)	0.41	0.41

   a i State what the current readings (x) and (y) would be. (1)

   x = _____ A   y = _____ A

   ii Explain why you think this. (1)

   b State and explain what the current reading (z) would be. (2)

3 a Use the information in tables 1 and 2 to calculate the overall resistance of:

  i circuit A (2)

  ii circuit B. (2)

b Describe how two bulbs can be put in a circuit to give the lowest possible overall resistance. (1)

Edexcel GCSE (9–1)
Combined Science

CP12a — Core practical 6: Investigating densities

Ships have a 'Plimsoll line' marked on them to show how far into the water they can sink without becoming unsafe. The safe level depends on the density of sea water.

Your teacher may watch to see if you can:
- take careful measurements.

Task 1 – Densities of solids
Method

A Find the mass of the solid. Write the name of the material and the mass of the object in a table.

B Stand a displacement can on the bench with its spout over a bowl. Fill the can with water until the water just starts to come out of the spout.

C Hold a measuring cylinder under the spout and carefully drop your object into the can.

D If your object floats, carefully push it down until all of it is under the water. Your finger should not be in the water.

E Stand the measuring cylinder on the bench and read the volume of water you have collected. This is the same as the volume of your object. Write the volume down.

Practical Objective
To compare the densities of different liquids and solids.

Apparatus
- balance
- displacement can
- measuring cylinder
- bowl
- solids

Safety
- Mop up any spills straight away.

The volume of the water displaced by an object is the same as the volume of the object.

Recording your results

1 Complete the table below.

Material	Mass (g)	Volume (cm³)	Density (g/cm³)

2 Calculate the density of each solid and write it in the table. The equation you need is shown. You will need to learn and recall this equation in your exam.

$$\text{density (g/cm}^3\text{)} = \frac{\text{mass (g)}}{\text{volume (cm}^3\text{)}}$$

Edexcel GCSE (9–1)
Combined Science
CP12a — Core practical 6: Investigating densities

Task 2 – Densities of liquids

Method

A Put an empty measuring cylinder on a balance and zero the balance.

B Carefully pour 50 cm³ of a liquid into the measuring cylinder. Write down the name of the liquid and the reading on the balance. This is the mass of 50 cm³ of the liquid.

Apparatus
- balance
- measuring cylinder
- beaker
- liquids

Safety
- Mop up any spills straight away.

Recording your results

1 Complete the table below.

Liquid	Mass of 50 cm³ (g)	Density (g/cm³)

2 Calculate the density of each liquid and write it in the table. You will need to learn and be able to recall the equation for how density is calculated. It is shown on the previous page.

Considering your results/conclusions

3 **a** What was the range of densities for the solids you measured?

_____
_____
_____
_____

b What was the range of densities for the liquids?

_____
_____
_____
_____

4 Compare the densities of the solids and liquids that you tested.

_____
_____
_____
_____
_____
_____

Edexcel GCSE (9–1)
Combined Science

CP12a Core practical 6: Investigating densities

Exam-style questions

1. Write down the equation for calculating the density of a substance. (1)

2. A student found that the mass of 50 cm³ (0.000 05 m³) of cooking oil was 46 g. Calculate the density of the cooking oil and state the unit. (2)

3. A large piece of wood is 2 m long, 50 cm wide and 2 cm thick. It has a mass of 12 kg. Calculate its density and state the unit. (3)

4. A student uses the method in the practical that you have completed and works out that the density of pure water is 980 kg/m³. A textbook gives a value of 1000 kg/m³.

    a Give a possible reason for the error in the student's result. (1)

    b Describe a way of making the measurement of the density of fluids more accurate. (1)

Edexcel GCSE (9–1) Combined Science — CP12b & c

Core practical 7: Investigating water, Part 1

Scientists monitoring the progress of glaciers need to understand the properties of water in its three forms: ice, liquid water and steam.

Part 1: Melting ice

Your teacher may watch to see if you can:
- take careful measurements
- work safely.

Method

A Place a thermometer carefully into a boiling tube. Fill the boiling tube with crushed ice, and place the tube in a beaker. Adjust the position of the themometer so that its bulb is in the middle of the ice.

B Put the beaker onto a tripod and gauze. Pour hot water from a kettle into the beaker and keep it warm using a Bunsen burner.

C Measure the temperature of the ice every minute and record your results in a table. Stop taking readings three minutes after all the ice has melted.

D Note the time at which the ice starts to melt and the time when it appears to be completely melted.

Practical Objective

To investigate how the temperature of ice changes as it melts.

Apparatus

- eye protection
- boiling tube
- beaker
- thermometer
- heat-resistant mat
- tripod and gauze
- Bunsen burner
- stop clock
- hot water
- crushed ice

Safety

- Wear eye protection.
- Take care when handling hot apparatus.

Recording your results

1 Complete the table below.

Time (min)	Temperature (°C)

Considering your results/conclusions

2 Draw a line graph to show your results using the axes on the right. Mark on your graph the time when the ice started to melt and the time when it had completely melted.

Temperature (°C)

Time (min)

3 Describe the shape of your graph.

---

4 Explain the shape of your graph using ideas about the way particles are arranged in solids and liquids, and what happens to particles when the state of a substance changes.

Evaluation

5 a What sources of systematic error could be present in your results?

---

b How could you avoid these errors?

---

6 a What sources of random error could there be in your results?

---

b How could you avoid these errors?

Edexcel GCSE (9–1) Combined Science — CP12b & c

Core practical 7: Investigating water, Part 1

Exam-style questions

1. Describe how the particles are arranged and held together in:

    a ice (you may draw a labelled diagram to help with your answer) (2)

    b liquid water (you may draw a labelled diagram to help with your answer). (2)

2. The table shows a set of results from the melting ice investigation. Plot a graph to present these results. Draw a line through the points, and identify any anomalous results. (5)

Time (min)	Temperature (°C)
0	−12
1	−6
2	−4
3	0
4	0
5	0
6	2
7	4
8	6

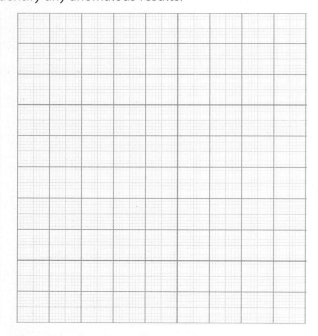

Edexcel GCSE (9–1) Combined Science — CP12b & c

Core practical 7: Investigating water, Part 2

Part 2: Specific heat capacity

Practical Objective
To find the specific heat capacity of water.

Apparatus
- polystyrene cup
- beaker
- tripod
- thermometer
- stop clock
- immersion heater
- joulemeter
- balance

Your teacher may watch to see if you can:
- take careful measurements.

Method

A Put a polystyrene cup in a beaker onto a balance and zero the balance. Then fill the cup almost to the top with water and write down the mass of the water. Carefully remove the cup from the balance.

B Put a thermometer in the water and support it as shown in the diagram. Put a 12 V electric immersion heater into the water, making sure the heating element is completely below the water level. Connect the immersion heater to a joulemeter.

C Record the temperature of the water and then switch the immersion heater on. Stir the water in the cup gently using the thermometer.

D After five minutes, record the temperature of the water again and also write down the reading on the joulemeter.

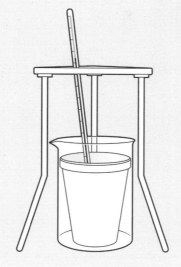

Recording your results

1 Record your results in this table.

Mass of water (g)	Mass of water (kg)	Starting temperature of water (°C)	Temperature after 5 minutes (°C)	Temperature change (°C)	Joulemeter reading (J)

Considering your results/conclusions

2 Divide the mass of water by 1000 to find the mass in kilograms. Write your answer in the table.

3 Subtract the temperature of the water after five minutes from the starting temperature to find the change in temperature. Write your answer in the table.

4 Calculate the specific heat capacity of water using this equation:

change in thermal energy* (J) = mass (kg) × specific heat capacity (J/kg °C) × change in temperature (°C)

You will need to select and apply this equation in the exam.

*Change in thermal energy is the same as energy transferred, and is measured using the joulemeter.

CP12b & c — Core practical 7: Investigating water, Part 2

Evaluation

5 Why did you use the glass beaker and the tripod?

6 Why did you put the water into a polystyrene cup instead of a beaker?

7 How would using a beaker have affected your results?

8 What are the possible sources of error in your investigation?

Edexcel GCSE (9–1) Combined Science — CP12b & c

Core practical 7: Investigating water, Part 2

Exam-style questions

1 State what is meant by the specific heat capacity of a substance. (1)

2 Sam heated 250 g of water in a polystyrene cup. The joulemeter reading was 11 kJ and the temperature change was 10 °C.

   a Calculate the specific heat capacity of water using the following equation:

$$\text{specific heat capacity (J/kg°C)} = \frac{\text{change in thermal energy (J)}}{\text{mass (kg)} \times \text{change in temperature (°C)}}$$

You will need to select and apply this equation in the exam. (3)

Specific heat capacity of water = _____ J/kg °C

   b A textbook gives the specific heat capacity of water as 4181 J/kg °C.
Suggest and explain why you would expect Sam's result to be higher than this. (3)

   c Suggest how the method described above could be improved to reduce these errors. (1)

Edexcel GCSE (9-1)
Combined Science

CP13a — Core practical 8: Investigating springs

Designers need to know the characteristics of springs so that they can choose the best spring for their purpose.

Your teacher may watch to see if you can:
- take careful measurements.

Method

A Set up the apparatus as shown in the diagram. The zero on the ruler should be level with the bottom of the unstretched spring.

B Measure the length of the spring with no masses hanging on it and write it down.

C Hang a 100 g mass on the spring. Record the extension of the spring (the length shown on the ruler).

D Repeat step **C** until you have found the extension of the spring with 10 different masses. Each 100 g mass puts a downwards force of 1 N on the spring.

E Repeat steps **A** to **D** for a different spring.

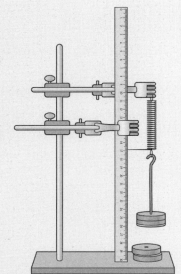

Practical Objective
To investigate the extension and work done when applying forces to a spring.

Apparatus
- eye protection
- stand and two clamps
- springs
- metre ruler
- masses

Safety
- Wear eye protection.

Recording your results

1 Draw a table like this to record your results.

	Spring 1		Spring 2	
Force (N)	Extension (cm)	Extension (m)	Extension (cm)	Extension (m)
0	0	0		
1				

2 Draw a graph to show force in newtons against extension in metres.
Put extension on the horizontal axis and force on the vertical axis. Plot points for all your springs on the same graph, join them with lines of best fit and identify any anomalous results.

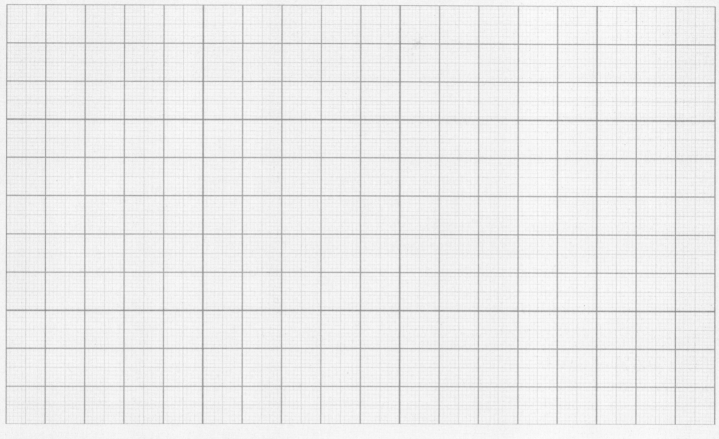

Considering your results/conclusions

3 Which of your springs feels the stiffest? (Which one takes more force to pull it?)

4 Calculate the gradient of the line on your graph for each spring. The gradient gives you the spring constant for each spring. The spring constant gives a measure of how stiff a spring is: the larger the spring constant, the stiffer the spring.

Edexcel GCSE (9–1)
Combined Science

CP13a Core practical 8: Investigating springs

5 How can you work out which springs should feel the stiffest by looking at their spring constants?

6 The work done to stretch a spring can be calculated using the following equation:

energy transferred in stretching (J) = $\frac{1}{2}$ × spring constant (N/m) × extension² (m)²

You will need to select and apply this equation in the exam.

Calculate the energy transferred in stretching each of the springs that you tested.

Edexcel GCSE (9–1) Combined Science

CP13a — Core practical 8: Investigating springs

Exam-style questions

1 a A student measures the extension of a spring while adding different masses (loading).
The student then measures the extension of the spring while removing the masses (unloading).
The student repeats the investigation using a rubber band instead of the spring.
The following table shows her results.

	Spring			Rubber band	
	Extension (mm)	Extension (mm)		Extension (mm)	Extension (mm)
Load (N)	Loading	Unloading	Load (N)	Loading	Unloading
0	0	0	0	0	0
1	20	20	1	14	25
2	40	40	2	33	42
3	60	60	3	60	60

State two similarities and two differences between the results for the spring and the results for the rubber band. **(4)**

Similarities

1. _____

2. _____

Differences

1. _____

2. _____

b A spring has an extension of 0.5 m when there is a force of 20 N pulling on it.

i Calculate the spring constant. **(2)**

ii Calculate the energy transferred in stretching this spring.
You will need to select and apply one of the equations on pages 95 and 96. **(2)**

Energy = _____ J

93

Edexcel GCSE (9–1) Combined Science

CP13a — Core practical 8: Investigating springs

2 A student carried out the investigation described, adding 10 N to the spring between each measurement. The spring stretched by only 1 mm with 10 N hanging on it.

   a Describe how this might affect the accuracy of the results. (2)

   b Explain how the method could be modified to improve the accuracy of the student's results. (2)

Edexcel GCSE (9–1)
Combined Science — Equations

Equations in the left hand column are ones you may be asked to *recall and apply* in your exam.

You do not need to recall the equations in the right hand column, but you should be able to select and apply them in an exam.

Equations for Higher tier only are marked with the Higher icon.

Recall and apply	Select and apply
Unit CP1 Motion distance travelled = average speed × time $d = x \times t$ acceleration = change in velocity ÷ time taken $a = \dfrac{(v - u)}{t}$	(final velocity)² − (initial velocity)² = 2 × acceleration × distance $v^2 - u^2 = 2 \times a \times s$
Unit CP2 Forces and motion force = mass × acceleration $F = m \times a$ weight = mass × gravitational field strength $W = m \times g$ **H** momentum = mass × velocity $p = m \times v$	**H** force = change in momentum ÷ time $F = \dfrac{(mv - mu)}{t}$
Unit CP3 Conservation of energy kinetic energy = ½ × mass × (speed)² $KE = \tfrac{1}{2} \times m \times v^2$ change in gravitational potential energy = mass × gravitational field strength × change in vertical height $GPE = m \times g \times h$ efficiency = $\dfrac{\text{useful energy transferred by the device}}{\text{total energy supplied to the device}}$	
Unit CP4 Waves wave speed = frequency × wavelength $v = f \times \lambda$ wave speed = distance ÷ time $v = \dfrac{x}{t}$	
Unit CP7 Energy – Forces doing work work done = force × distance moved in the direction of the force $E = F \times d$ power = work done ÷ time taken $P = \dfrac{E}{t}$	
Unit CP9 Forces and their effects moment of a force = force × distance normal to the direction of the force	

Edexcel GCSE (9–1)
Combined Science — Equations

Recall and apply

Unit CP9 Electricity and circuits

charge = current × time
$$Q = I \times t$$

energy transferred = charge moved × potential difference
$$E = Q \times V$$

potential difference = current × resistance
$$V = I \times R$$

power = energy transferred ÷ time taken
$$P = \frac{E}{t}$$

electrical power = current × potential difference
$$P = I \times V$$

electrical power = current squared × resistance
$$P = I^2 \times R$$

Unit CP10 Magnetism and the motor effect

Unit CP11 Electromagnetic induction

Unit CP12 Particle model

density = mass ÷ volume
$$\rho = \frac{m}{V}$$

Unit CP13 Forces and matter

force exerted on a spring = spring constant × extension
$$F = k \times x$$

Select and apply

Unit CP9 Electricity and circuits

energy transferred = current × potential difference × time
$$E = I \times V \times t$$

Unit CP10 Magnetism and the motor effect

H force on a conductor at right angles to a magnetic field carrying a current = magnetic flux density × current × length
$$F = B \times I \times l$$

Unit CP11 Electromagnetic induction

For transformers with 100% efficiency,

potential difference across primary coil × current in primary coil = potential difference across secondary coil × current in secondary coil
$$V_p \times I_p = V_s \times I_s$$

Unit CP12 Particle model

change in thermal energy = mass × specific heat capacity × change in temperature
$$\Delta Q = m \times c \times \Delta\theta$$

thermal energy for a change of state = mass × specific latent heat
$$Q = M \times L$$

to calculate pressure or volume for gases of fixed mass at constant temperature
$$P_1 \times V_1 = P_2 \times V_2$$

Unit CP13 Forces and matter

energy transferred in stretching = 0.5 × spring constant × (extension)²
$$E = \tfrac{1}{2} \times k \times x^2$$

Edexcel GCSE (9–1)
Combined Science — Glossary

Word	Meaning
accuracy	How close a value is to its real value.
anomalous	Does not fit a pattern.
caution	Means 'beware'.
chemical reaction	A change in which one or more new substances are formed.
chromatogram	The results of chromatography (e.g. a dried piece of paper for paper chromatography), when the dissolved solids have been separated.
circuit diagram	A diagram drawn with standard symbols and straight lines to represent an electrical circuit.
column graph	Another term for 'bar chart'.
control variables	Variables whose values need to be kept steady during an investigation.
correlation	A relationship between two variables. If an increase in is linked to an increase in the other, it is 'positive'. An increase in one linked to a decrease in the other is 'negative'.
data	Observations or measurements collected in investigations.
decimal places	The number of digits after the decimal point.
dependent variable	The variable that is measured in an investigation. The values of the dependent variable depend on those of the independent variable.
directly proportional relationship	A relationship between two variables where one variable doubles when the other doubles. The graph is a straight line through (0,0). We say that one variable is directly proportional to the other.
discrete data	Data given in the form of limited values. For example, shoe sizes come in whole sizes and half sizes but not in sizes in between. So size 4, size 4½ and size 5 are all possible, but size 4.149 is not. The number of different shoe sizes is limited.
estimate	An approximate answer, often calculated from a sample or using rounded values.
evidence	Data used to support an idea or show that it is wrong.
extension	The length by which a material extends or is compressed when a certain force is applied. It is the length of the material after the application of the force minus the original length.
hazard	Something that could cause harm.
hazard symbol	A warning symbol that shows why something can cause harm.
hypothesis	An idea about how something works that can be tested using experiments. The plural is *hypotheses*.
independent variable	The variable that you chose the values of in an investigation.
interval	The gap between one value of an independent variable and the next, in an investigation.
linear relationship	A relationship between variables that produces a straight line when plotted on a scatter graph. The line does *not* have to go through the (0,0) point.
line graph	A graph used to show how a variable changes with time.
line of best fit	A line going through a set of points on a graph, so that roughly equal numbers of points end up on either side of the line.
mean	An average calculated by adding up the values of a set of measurements and dividing by the number of measurements in the set.
median	The middle value in a set of values that has been written in order.
mode	The most common value in a set of values.
model	A way of showing or representing a phenomenon that helps you to think about it or to investigate it.
outlier	Another term for 'anomalous reading'.

# Edexcel GCSE (9–1) Combined Science — Glossary and Answers

peer review	An evaluation of the quality of a scientific paper carried out by other scientists conduct research in the same area of science.
precision	How close a set of repeated measurements are to one another.
prediction	What you think will happen in an experiment.
qualitative data	Data that is not in form of numbers (e.g. the names of colours).
random error	A mistake made in a measurement, which can be different every time that measurement is made.
range	The highest and lowest values in a set of data.
relationship	A link between two variables.
repeatable	Results that are similar when repeated by the same experimenter. You can be more certain that a set of repeatable results is correct.
reproducible	Results that are similar when repeated by different experimenters.
risk	The chance of harm being caused by a hazard.
sample	To take a small part of something to investigate. You use a sample to draw conclusions about the larger whole.
scatter graph	A graph in which data for two variables are plotted as points. This allows you to see whether there is a relationship between the two variables.
significant figures	The number of digits of a value, starting from the first non-zero digit.
systematic error	An error that is the same for all readings, such as forgetting to zero a balance before using it to measure a series of masses.
theory	A hypothesis (or set of hypotheses) that has been repeatedly confirmed through experiment and for which there is a high degree of agreement in the scientific community.
trial run	A quick, rough version of an experiment that is carried out to ensure that the main experiment is designed well.
variable	Anything that can change and be measured.

CB1b

Exam-style questions

1 a The lens makes things appear two times bigger. (1)
   b $2 \times 7 = \times 14$, $5 \times 7 = \times 35$, $10 \times 7 = \times 70$. (3)
2 Place the slide on the stage of the microscope and look through the eyepiece lens. (1) Plus two from: Turn the focusing wheel to obtain a clear image, (1) start at the lowest lens magnification, (1) increase the magnification of the objective lens and refocus using the focusing wheel. (1)
3 $0.80\,\text{mm}/400$ (1) $= 0.002\,\text{mm}$ (1) $= 2\,\mu\text{m}$. (1) Full marks for correct numerical answer without working. (1) for working when answer incorrect.

CB1g

1 Your own prediction and explanation.
2 Your own table.
3 Your own data.
4 Your own graph.
5 Your own results, e.g. the closer the pH is to 7, the less the time taken for amylase to digest starch.
6 Your own results, e.g. 7 is the optimum pH. At pHs below and above this pH, the shape of the active site is affected and so the enzyme does not work so well.
7–10 Your own results.

Exam-style questions

1 a Gas syringe (1) with any suitable reason, such as some of the oxygen might dissolve in water (if the upturned measuring cylinder was used), or the scale on the syringe might be finer so giving more accurate readings. (1)
   b Use a pH meter (1) because:
   - universal/pH indicator solution might interfere with the reaction
   - OR a pH meter is more accurate
   - OR universal/pH indicator is not accurate/sensitive enough to distinguish between small pH increments. (1)

   c Graph drawn from data in table:
   - axes drawn with suitable scales and labelled appropriately (1)
   - points plotted accurately and joined by one curved line for each pH (1)
   - both lines drawn on same axes. (1)

   d Measurement taken at 4 min for pH 6 is too low compared to the rest of the results. (1) Any suitable reason that explains the low result, such as scale was not read accurately. (1)
   e $10.6\,\text{cm}^3$ produced in 6 min $= \dfrac{10.6}{6} = 1.77\,\text{cm}^3/\text{min}$ (1)

2 a Bacterium A: pH 4 (1); bacterium B: pH 2. (1)
   b The enzyme from bacterium A (1) because it takes less time to break down the substrate than the enzyme from bacterium B. (1)
   c Bacterium B (1) because its optimum pH is the most acidic. (1)

CB1h

1 Your own predictions and explanations.
2 Your own table.
3 Your own results.
4 Your own results.
5 Your own results.
6 Your own results.
7 Your own graph.
8 Description of your own graph. There should be a small increase in mass for the 0% solution and then increasing reductions in mass for the 40%, 80% and 100% solutions.
9 Explanation of your own graph. Likely answers would be that, for the 0% solution, the solution has a higher water concentration than the potato strip, so the potato strip absorbs water by osmosis. For the 40%, 80% and 100% solutions, the

Edexcel GCSE (9–1)
Combined Science — Answers

concentration of water in the potato strip is higher than the concentration of water in the solutions, so water will move from the potato strip to the solution by osmosis.

10 The percentage change in mass gives an indication of the overall movement of molecules between the potato strips and the solution.

11 A mean value is likely to 'smooth out' any variations in the way the experiment was carried out.

12 Your own results.

Exam-style questions

1 a A + 0.09 g; B − 0.26 g; C − 0.55 g; D − 1.17 g (1 mark for all correct values, 1 mark for units and correctly identifying gain or loss).
   b A + 1.9%; B − 5.0%; C − 11.1%; D − 24.1% (1 mark for all correct values, 1 mark for units and correctly identifying gain or loss).
   c The slice gained mass because osmosis took place into the potato from the surrounding water. (1)
   d All the slices lost mass, but the percentage loss in mass increased as the solution concentration increased. (1) This is because osmosis happens faster as the difference in concentration between the potato tissue and solution increases. (1)
   e A concentration equivalent to between 0% and 10% sucrose solution, (1) because when the concentrations are equal there will be no change in mass. (1)
   f Any suitable suggestion that identifies how accuracy can be increased, such as using a range of solutions between 0% and 10%. (1)

2 a The potato lost water fastest, (1) because the gradient of its line is steeper than for the halophyte. (1)
   b Potato has a lower solute concentration inside its cells than the halophyte, (1) so will lose water faster by osmosis than the halophyte when placed in a concentrated solution. (1)
   c Rate of change = $\frac{-5.6}{4}$ = −1.4% per minute. (1)

CB6b

1 Your own results.
2 a Your own results.   b Your own results.
3 Your own graph.
4 a Your own results.   b Your own results.
5 The part of an experiment in which the *independent* variable is not applied is called the control. A control is used to check that the *independent* variable has an effect (and that the effect is not due to another variable). In this experiment, the independent variable is the *light* intensity. The control is the *tube covered in foil*. We know that the independent variable has a direct effect on the final pH of the indicator because *when light could not get to the algae, the indicator colour did not change* [or words to that effect].

Exam-style question

1 a At about 2 minutes – after this time, oxygen concentration rises, as it is produced by photosynthesis when it is light. (1)
   b At about 13 minutes – after this time, oxygen concentration falls, as photosynthesis stops producing it and respiration uses it up. (1)
   c Working shown (2) to work out the gradient of the line of best fit, e.g.:
   $$\frac{5.96 - 5.3}{12 - 2.5} = \frac{0.66}{9.5} = 0.07 \text{ mg/dm}^3/\text{min} \quad (1)$$
   d $y = 0.07 \times 4.333 + 5.1$ (2) = 5.4 mg dm^3 (1)
   e Photosynthesis needs light (1), and the greater the light intensity (1), the faster the rate of photosynthesis. (1)
   f The light intensity is not the limiting factor (1) / but something else **is** a limiting factor. (1)
   g Either increase carbon dioxide concentration or increase temperature. (1)

CB8d

1 Your own results.
2 Your own graph.
3 a The temperature.
   b The distance moved by the coloured liquid.
   c One of: the number of organisms, the length of time that the coloured liquid was observed to move.
   d The number of organisms – because the higher number you have, the higher the rate of respiration (or vice versa with a lower number); the length of time – because this will not allow you to compare readings if the timing is different.
   e The greater the temperature, the faster the rate of respiration.
   f Chemical reactions occur more quickly at higher temperatures.
4 a oxygen
   b carbon dioxide
   c it is absorbed by the soda lime

Exam-style questions

1 Not below freezing (since this may harm the cells of the organisms) (1 mark – for both the temperature and the reason). Not above 40 °C (accept a range of 30–45 °C) since the organisms are unlikely to experience these temperatures in reality/ their enzymes may start to denature/may cause injury to the organisms (1 mark – for both the temperature and the reason).
2 a To increase the likelihood that the results are correct. (1)
   b Correctly plotted points, (1) graph with suitable axes and labels. (1)
   c 30 °C, 10 mm. (1)
   d A leak in the container allowing air into it, **or** starting the stop clock too late/stopping it too early. (1)
   e Line of best fit. (1)
   f The higher the temperature, the greater the rate of respiration/the faster the coloured liquid moves. (1)
   g At higher temperatures, organisms/enzymes are more active (1), so more respiration is needed to release energy. (1)

CB9b

1 Your own results.
2 Your own graph.
3–7 Your own results.

Exam-style questions

1 Quadrats placed along the transect will record changes in presence/absence or changes in abundance from one area to another. (1)
2 Factors caused by physical and chemical differences in the environment. (1)
3 Any two suitable abiotic factors with a reason (max. 2 marks, 1 for each factor), such as:
   - air humidity may be greater under the tree than in open air, because it is cooler and there is less wind under the tree
   - soil moisture may be greater in open ground than under the tree, because tree roots absorb a lot of moisture and canopy shelters ground
   - air temperature may vary more above open ground than under the tree because the tree canopy provides shelter.
4 Any answer which indicates that different species are adapted to different habitats, (1) and so distribution and abundance will be affected by abiotic factors that vary from their preferred habitat. (1)
5 a Sufficient number of quadrats used, (1) count the number of daisy plants in each quadrat, (1) use the mean number of daisy plants, area of quadrat and area of field to estimate population. (1)
   b 147 (2) Full marks for correct numerical answer with/without working. If answer is incorrect allow 1 mark for 350/0.50 = 700.

CC2d Part 1

1 The liquid you have produced (the distillate) will be clear and colourless, the ink colour should not appear in the distillate.
2 The answer should be around 100 °C as this is the boiling point of water; however, values slightly below 100 °C are acceptable providing the reason given links to impurities.
3 To keep the test tube cool (and condense the vapour back into a liquid).
4 a The glass might smash and therefore there are risk of cuts; boiling water could spill and risk of this going onto clothes and skin; people could slip due to spilt water on the floor.
   b Stand up while doing practical work; so that you can more easily move out of the way; make sure that the tripod is stable and that the flask is steady; use a clamp and stand to secure the flask in place.

Edexcel GCSE (9–1) Combined Science — Answers

5. Any suitable hazard; together with one way of reducing the risk – e.g. hazard from liquid boiling over; reducing the risk could include the use of anti-bumping granules.

6. **a** Air hole closed (yellow flame); makes the flame more visible (luminous); so reducing the risk of someone touching the flame accidentally. The gas tap should be fully on, to avoid the flame being blown out.
   b Air hole slightly/half open; gas tap turned about half on; makes sure heating is gentle; helps to reduce the risk of the liquid boiling over and avoids depositing soot onto the gauze/flask.

7. Your answer should refer to your actual results and how well this compared to the success criteria you set out in Q1 above. Possible tests for water could be: adding the distillate to anhydrous copper sulfate which turns blue (with water) or using cobalt chloride paper which turns purple/pink (with water).

8. Your answer should include:
   - ink/liquid is heated until it boils
   - liquid/water evaporates and turns into steam, also known as water vapour
   - steam is pure water vapour, so the temperature reading on the thermometer is 100 °C
   - the steam/vapour passes into the condenser, where it cools down
   - when it cools it turns from a vapour/gas back into a liquid
   - the pure water collects as the distillate

Exam-style questions

1. **a** It becomes darker (1) because it becomes more concentrated/solvent leaves the ink but the coloured substances do not. (1)
   b The liquid being distilled is a mixture containing water and ink. Only the water boils; the boiling point of water is 100 °C. (1)

2. Solvent has a lower boiling point than the solute/solvent is liquid, but solute is solid at room temperature (1); solvent boils and leaves the solution (1); solvent vapour is cooled and condensed away from the solution. (1)

3. Heat the liquid until it boils (1); measure its boiling point (1); pure water boils at 100 °C. (1)

CC2d Part 2

1. You should have correctly identified different colours in the inks you tested.
2. You should have correctly measured from the pencil line to where the solvent reached.
3. You should have completed the middle rows of your results table.
4. You should have completed the bottom row of your results table; you needed to use the formula to work out the R_f values.
5. This is dependent on your results; you need to look for any black inks which did not separate into a number of colours – the ink just remained as one main dot. Remember, the inks must have moved otherwise they would be insoluble in water.
6. Again, this is dependent on your results. However, similar coloured dyes (in the same location) on your chromatography paper are likely to contain the same chemical compound.
7. The graphite from the pencil will not dissolve in the solvent (water) and so will not interfere with the results. The line will also help when working out the R_f values, as there will be a clear point to take measurements from.
8. This was done so you could easily recall which pen/original colour of ink was used to produce each spot of ink.
9. The water rises up the paper, and dissolves the dyes.
10. This was done to stop the dyes washing out of the paper.
11. The answer will depend on how clear the top level of each dye is on your chromatograms; if it is difficult to identify the top of each dye accurately, then the accuracy and reliability of the calculated R_f values will be reduced.

Exam-style questions

1. **a** Propanone. (1)
   b Paper. (1)
   c She should avoid flames because propanone is flammable. (1)
   d The ink would dissolve into the propanone/wash out of the paper. (1)

2. **a** Ink X is a mixture of inks B and C (1) and does not contain ink A. (1)
   b You would need to use this formula:
   $$R_f = \frac{\text{distance moved by the compound}}{\text{distance moved by the solvent}}$$
   and either measure the distances on the chromatogram or use the scale at the side.
   $R_f = 0.75$ (1 mark for substitution in formula, 1 mark for final answer)

3. 5.50/9.15 (1); = 0.60109 (1); to 2 significant figures = 0.60. (1) Correct answer = 3 marks.

CC8c

1. The crystals are blue and diamond shaped. (The size will vary depending on conditions.)
2. **a** clear solution
   b black solid (powder)
   c blue solution
3. copper oxide + sulfuric acid → copper sulfate + water
4. So that all the acid is used up.
5. The acid would react with the excess copper oxide and some or all of it would disappear.
6. Copper oxide.
7. Copper sulfate.
8. Because the hydrogen ions of the acid are removed (and a salt and water are formed).
9. Copper oxide.
10. $CuO(s) + H_2SO_4(aq) \rightarrow CuSO_4(aq) + H_2O(l)$

Exam-style questions

1. Because it is formed by the reaction between a base and an acid. (1)
2. The copper(II) oxide is a solid (made up of larger particles) that gets stuck in the filter paper. (1) The particles of the copper sulfate are in solution (smaller) so pass through the filter paper. (1)
3. **a** nickel oxide + hydrochloric acid → nickel chloride + water (1)
   b $NiO(s) + 2HCl(aq)$ (1) $\rightarrow NiCl_2(aq) + H_2O(l)$ (1)
4. Place the solution in an evaporating basin (1) and heat over a beaker half full of water until about half the liquid has evaporated. (1) When cool (1) place the remaining liquid in a watch glass for a few days. (1)
5. Small crystals are produced by fast evaporation of the water in the solution. (1) Large crystals are produced by slow evaporation of the water in the solution. (1)

CC8d

1. Suitable table drawn: two columns; first column labelled mass of $Ca(OH)_2$ powder added/(g); second column labelled pH of the mixture; sufficient rows for nine readings.
2. Graph plotted with pH on vertical axis, mass of $Ca(OH)_2$ added (g) on horizontal axis; curve of best fit drawn; suitable title included.
3. Expected results: pH increases as more calcium hydroxide is added; end-point is 1.85 g; maximum solubility of $Ca(OH)_2$ has been reached; so beyond this excess $Ca(OH)_2$ is seen.
4. Intercept at pH 7 identified; mass read from graph.
5. Improvement suggested, e.g. use more precise balance (±0.01 g or ±0.001 g); increase volume of acid used; use narrow range indicator paper; use pH meter.

Exam-style questions

1. **a** calcium chloride (1)
   b $Ca(OH)_2(s) + 2HCl(aq) \rightarrow CaCl_2(aq) + 2H_2O(l)$ (1 mark for formulae, 1 mark for balancing, 1 mark for state symbols)
2. To avoid damage to eyes (1) because hydrochloric acid is irritant/corrosive. (1)
3. **a** Volume of acid (1); concentration of acid. (1)
   b pH of reaction mixture. (1)
   c Use a thermometer instead of indicator paper or a pH meter. (1)
4. **a** To make sure that it gives an accurate pH value / pH value close to the true value. (1)

Edexcel GCSE (9–1)
Combined Science — Answers

b The pH meter has the higher resolution because it gives readings to 1 or 2 decimal places (1) but universal indicator paper only gives readings to the nearest whole pH unit. (1)

CC10a
Method 1
1. Your table should be complete, including the columns showing the change in mass.
2. Your graph should show change in mass of electrode on the vertical axis and current on the horizontal axis; these axes need to be labelled (including units). You should have chosen a suitable scale that enables the graph to be as large as possible, and the points need to be plotted correctly with a line of best fit which is straight. The line for the anode should show a decrease in mass and the line for the cathode should show an increase in mass as the current increases.
3. For the anode: the decrease in mass is directly proportional to the current, **or** as the current increases, the mass decreases proportionally.
   For the cathode: the increase in mass is directly proportional to the current, **or** as the current increases, the mass increases proportionally.
4. Anode: copper atoms lose electrons to form copper ions; the copper ions dissolve in the solution, **or** $Cu(s) \rightarrow Cu^{2+}(aq) + 2e$
   Cathode: copper ions gain electrons to form copper; which sticks to the surface of the cathode, **or** $Cu^{2+}(aq) + 2e \rightarrow Cu(s)$
5. Your prediction should be made by reading from 0.35 A on the horizontal axis, reading/drawing a line up to the best fit line for the *anode* you drew and then reading/drawing a line across to the change in mass of electrode on the vertical axis.
6. Some of the deposited copper does not stick to the cathode, so the cathode does not gain as much mass as expected, **or** there are impurities in the anode and they fall to the bottom of the beaker, so the anode appears to lose more mass.
7. You would need to repeat the experiment and take an average of the concordant results.

Method 2
1. At the anode: bubbles of a colourless gas, product is oxygen.
   At the cathode: covered with a layer of brown metal, product is copper.
2. Hydroxide ions from the water are attracted to the anode; they lose electrons to form oxygen and water.
   Copper ions are attracted to the cathode; they gain two electrons to form copper.
3. **H** $4OH^- \rightarrow O_2 + 2H_2O + 4e$ oxidation
   $Cu^{2+} + 2e \rightarrow Cu$ reduction

Exam-style questions
1. As it is a four-mark question, four statements are needed in order to gain full marks. The answer should include:
   - sulfate and hydroxide ions are attracted to the anode during electrolysis (1)
   - hydroxide ions are more readily discharged than sulfate ions (1)
   - so oxygen is produced (1)
   - as there are no copper atoms in the graphite electrode to form ions. (1)
2. **a** Any sensible precaution would be allowed (1), but typical answers could be:
   - wear eye protection, to prevent copper sulfate solution splashing into eyes
   - ensure no naked flames when using propanone, as it is flammable
   - ensure the power supply does not go above 6 V, to prevent the connecting wires and electrodes from getting too hot.

   b So that the copper deposited will adhere to the cathode. (1)
   c The current may vary during the experiment and the variable resistor can be used to keep the current constant. (1)
   d To remove the copper sulfate solution. (1)
   e To help the electrodes to dry more quickly as it evaporates quickly. (1)

CC14a & b Part 1
1. If results are good, the graph should show two curves rising steadily and levelling off at about the same point. The curve for the small chips should rise and level off more quickly.
2. The reactions had finished when the graph levelled off.
3. For a fixed mass of chips, the smaller the chips, the larger the surface area (to volume ratio).
4. The larger the surface area (to volume ratio), the faster the reaction.
5. The graph for larger surface area to volume ratio (smaller chips) rises more quickly at the start and levels off more quickly. Therefore, the larger the surface area, the faster the reaction.
6. If the results are good, the graph should show a straight line rising steadily as the concentration increases.
7. The higher the concentration of the acid, the faster the reaction.
8. The graph for volume of gas produced in one minute against concentration rises steadily. Therefore, the higher the concentration, the faster the reaction.
9. Possible sources of error are: measuring the volume of gas (which is difficult because of the bubbles in the measuring cylinder), and making sure the marble chips are all the same size. (Other answers possible.)
10. Measure the volume of gas produced for a longer time, or measure larger volumes of gas. (Other answers possible.)

Exam-style question
1. **Level 3** (5–6 marks): shows accurate and relevant chemical understanding throughout a response showing full understanding of scientific ideas, enquiry, techniques and procedures. A clear structure is shown which can easily be followed.
   Level 2 (3–4 marks): shows chemical understanding which is relevant, including understanding of scientific ideas and enquiry, techniques and procedures. Has a structure which is mostly clear and logical.
   Level 1 (1–2 marks): simple description with little detail, but with some structure and coherence.
   (No marks): no relevant content.
   Indicative content (maximum 6 marks):
   Apparatus: eye protection, conical flask, delivery tube and bung, gas syringe or 100 cm³ measuring cylinder and water trough, balance, stop clock, magnesium carbonate powder, dilute sulfuric acid of a range of concentrations, measuring cylinder.
   Method: Weigh magnesium carbonate, add to flask, add stated volume of sulfuric acid, record volume of gas produced at regular time intervals. Use the same mass of magnesium carbonate in each part of the experiment.
   Repeat for a range of concentrations of sulfuric acid.

CC14a & b Part 2
1. There should be a completed table of results with two columns: one for temperature, and the other for the time taken for the cross to disappear. The correct units should also be clearly displayed in the table.
2. The graph should show a curve, with time decreasing quickly as temperature increases.
3. **a** The rate increases quickly as the temperature increases.
   b The graph shows that as the temperature rises, the time for the reaction decreases; this means the rate of reaction increases.
4. The time taken would halve.
5. **a** 10 °C.
   b You need to mark on your graph a particular temperature – for example, 40 °C. From this you draw a line to the time taken axis and make a note of this value. You need to halve this time; for example, if your result was 60 seconds, you need to look at the temperature at 30 seconds. From this, you should be able to see a temperature difference of about 10 °C.
6. Any two of the following measurements: temperature, time and volume of solutions.
7. Errors with recording temperature and time could be reduced by repeating the experiment more often. Errors with measuring

Edexcel GCSE (9–1)
Combined Science — Answers

volume of solution could be reduced by using burettes and/or pipettes. (Other answers possible.)

Exam-style questions

1. The powdered chalk has a larger surface area to volume ratio than the lumps of chalk. (1) This means more frequent collisions occur between the acid particles and the chalk. (1) More frequent collisions mean that the reaction occurs more quickly. (1)
2. a The cross disappears because the precipitate (solid) settles at the bottom of the flask. (1)
   b Vertical axis: 'Time for cross to disappear (s)' (1); horizontal axis: 'Average temperature (°C)' (1); sketch shows line starting high and curving downwards, getting less steep as it gets closer to the horizontal axis. (1)
   c As the temperature increases the time taken decreases (1), so the reaction is getting quicker as less time is needed to get to the same point (an approximate 10 °C rise in temperature halves the time taken, so doubles the reaction rate). (1)
   d By repeating the experiment (at the same temperatures) and averaging the results. (1)

CP2d
1. Your own results.
2. Your own results.
3. Your own results.
4. Your own results.
5. Your own graph.
6. a Acceleration decreases as mass increases. (Acceleration is inversely proportional to mass, although you cannot determine that the relationship *is* one of inverse proportion without plotting a graph of acceleration against 1/mass and obtaining a straight line.)
   b Your own prediction.
7. a Your own results.
   b Your own results.
8. Your own results.
9. Your own results.

Exam-style questions

1. Acceleration is a change in speed over time (1), so find the difference in the two speeds and divide by the time taken to move between the two light gates. (1)
2. The acceleration is proportional to the force. (1)
3. The acceleration gets less as the mass increases. (1) *You should not write 'the acceleration is inversely proportional to the mass' at this point, as this cannot be determined for certain from the shape of the graph.*
4. Any two relevant readings from the graph (1); use of $F = m \times a$ (1) accept 8/4 etc.; mass = 2 kg (1); allow all 3 marks for 2 kg without working shown.

CP4b Part 1
1. Your own results.
2. Your own results.
3. Results may vary because of different water depths (and different frequencies/wavelengths for the measurement of the series of waves).
4. There may be less than one wave in a second/any errors in counting the waves are spread out over 10 s, so this will give a more accurate value.
5. Comments are likely to mention the difficulty of measuring the wavelength while the waves were moving. The camera 'freezes' the motion of the waves so it is easier to take a precise and accurate measurement.
6. Comments are likely to relate to the speed of the wave; difficult to measure an accurate time when something is moving fast. Suggestions could include using a video camera with a time also displayed.

CP4b Part 2
1. Your own results.
2. Your own results.
3. You could justify either answer: the wavelength, as this is obtained from a static measurement of the rod; the frequency, as this is measured electronically.
4. Your own table.
5. The sound travels too fast to use a stop clock/human reaction time would introduce errors greater than the time being measured.

Exam-style questions

1. a wave speed = frequency × wavelength (1)
   b $\text{speed} = \dfrac{\text{distance}}{\text{time}} = \dfrac{660 \text{ m}}{2 \text{ s}}$ (1) = 330 m/s (1)
2. wavelength = $\dfrac{1482 \text{ m/s}}{100 \text{ Hz}}$ (1) = 14.82 m = 15 m (1) to 2 significant figures
3. Use a stop clock to find how long it takes one wave to go from one buoy to the other (1) and calculate the speed by dividing 20 m by the measured time. (1)
4. a Description to include:
      make a (loud) sound next to one microphone (1), measure the time difference (from one microphone to the other) (1), measure the distance between the two microphones (1), divide the distance by the time (to measure the speed of sound) (1)
   b time interval is (very) small (1); eliminates/reduces effect of human reaction time (1) (note human error is not enough for this mark)

CP5a
1. Your own table.
2. Your own graph.
3. Your own results.
4. Your own results.
5. Your own conclusion.
6. a Your own results.
   b Your own results.

Exam-style questions

1. Light travels more slowly/at a different speed in glass. (1)
2. a Graph with sensible scales on axes (1) and axes labelled. (1) All points correctly plotted to ± half a square. (1) Smooth curve passing through all the points except the anomalous result. (1) Anomalous result (45°) identified. (1)
   b The angle of refraction increases as the angle of incidence increases (1), but the angle of refraction is always less than the angle of incidence. (1) The relationship between the angles of incidence and refraction is not a linear/proportional relationship. (1)
   c The answer should be 9.5° (from the values supplied for plotting the graph), accept ± 1°. (1)
3. The student may not have measured the angles accurately/may not have drawn the normal correctly. (1)

CP9e
1. A completed results table for both resistor and filament lamp.
2. The graph should show a straight line through the origin for the resistor, although a curve will be seen if the wires in the experiment got hot. There should be a curve (the slope of the line becoming shallower at higher potential difference values) for the filament lamp.
3. a The values for the resistor require the table to be read accurately and the values obtained substituted into the resistance equation correctly.
   b The values for the filament lamp require the table to be read accurately and the values obtained substituted into the resistance equation correctly.

Edexcel GCSE (9–1) Combined Science — Answers

  c As the potential difference increases, the resistance of the resistor stays the same – but the resistance of the filament lamp increases with increasing potential difference.

  d The graph for the resistor is a straight line through the origin, which means that current is proportional to potential difference and so the resistance is the same for all values of potential difference. You may also refer to the resistance calculations you carried out for 1 V and 6 V power pack settings.

  The graph for the filament lamp shows that the current is not proportional to the potential difference. As the potential difference increases, the current does increase but the change in current gets less and less for each increase in potential difference. This shows that the resistance increases as the potential difference increases.

4 a This is your own opinion as to how close your points are to your line of best fit.

  b The answers should refer to better quality data producing points that lie close to the line of best fit.

5 This is your own opinion as to how reproducible your results were. You need to compare with at least three other groups before coming to a final conclusion.

6 a In circuit Y the ammeter reading will be constant but in circuit Z the ammeters will measure different current values.

  b In circuit Y the voltmeter readings V1 and V2 will sum to the value of V3. In circuit Z the voltmeter readings V5 and V6 will be the same as V4.

7 Completed results table.

8 a The current through each filament lamp in parallel should be twice the current measured in circuit B.

  b The potential difference across each filament lamp in parallel should be twice the potential difference across each lamp when they are in series.

9 Increasing the potential difference across the supply changes the resistance of the filament lamps. This should not affect how the potential differences across the circuits compare, but may mean that the current through A3 and A4 is twice that of A1 only for lower potential difference settings, and is less than twice A1 at higher potential difference settings.

10 If fixed resistors are used, changing the potential difference across each circuit should not affect the comparisons, because the resistance does not change with potential difference.

Exam-style questions

1 Ohms (or Ω). (1)

2 a i Both should be 0.23 A (1)

  ii because the current is the same everywhere in a series circuit. (1)

  b 0.82 A (1) because the current through the power pack/cell is the sum of the currents in the branches of the circuit. (1)

3 a i $R = 4\,V / 0.23\,A$ (1) $= 17.4\,\Omega$ (1)

  ii $R = 4\,V / 0.82\,A$ (1) $= 4.9\,\Omega$ (1)

  b Connect them in parallel. (1)

CP12a

1 Your own results.
2 Your own results.
3 Your own results.
4 Your own results.

5 a & b The range of densities for the solids tested is likely to have been greater than the range of densities for the liquids.

6 The answer depends on the materials tested. Answers could point out that in general, solids are more dense than liquids, although there are some solids that are less dense. Very good answers may also suggest whether each solid will float or sink in the different liquids tested.

Exam-style questions

1 density $= \dfrac{\text{mass}}{\text{volume}}$ (or $\rho = m/V$) (1)

2 density $= 0.046\,\text{kg}/0.000\,05\,\text{m}^3$ (1) $= 920$ (1) kg/m^3 (1); also allow: $46\,\text{g}/50\,\text{cm}^3$ (1) $= 0.92$ (1) g/cm^3 (1)

3 volume $= 2\,\text{m} \times 0.5\,\text{m} \times 0.02\,\text{m} = 0.02\,\text{m}^3$ (1)

  density $= 2\,\text{kg}/0.02\,\text{m}^3$ (1) $= 100\,\text{kg/m}^3$ (1); also allow answer in g/cm^3 ($2000\,\text{g}/20\,000\,\text{cm}^3 = 0.1\,\text{g/cm}^3$)

4 a The measured mass was too low **or** the measured volume was too high (1) ('a measurement error' is not an acceptable answer).

  b Any sensible suggestion, such as: use a measuring cylinder with more accurate markings; zero the balance with the measuring cylinder on it and pour the liquid into that, so no liquid is left behind in the measuring cylinder. (1)

CP12b & c Part 1

1 Your own results.

2 Graphs should show an increase in temperature, a horizontal section while the ice is melting, and then a further rise in temperature as the water begins to warm up.

3 Description will depend on your own results.

4 As the ice is heated the particles move faster and the temperature rises. Eventually the temperature reaches the melting point of the substance and the energy from the water bath is being used to break the bonds holding the particles together in the solid. The temperature remains constant while this is happening. When all the ice has melted, the particles in the liquid move around faster as they get more energy, so the temperature rises again.

5 a Sources of systematic errors could be a faulty thermometer, or the thermometer not immersed fully in the substance being tested.

  b Check the thermometer against a known pair of temperatures (e.g. in ice and in boiling water), or compare it with another thermometer.

6 a Suggestions could include not reading the thermometer at the correct time, not recording the reading correctly, or using the thermometer incorrectly (e.g. by taking it out of the substance to read the temperature).

  b Answers depend on the errors suggested in **6a**. Any sensible methods of reducing errors are acceptable.

Exam-style questions

1 a Ice is a solid, so the particles are held in a fixed arrangement (1) by strong forces. (1) Allow full marks for a correctly labelled diagram.

  b Any two from: the forces between particles are not as strong as in ice/a solid (1) so the particles can move around (1) within the liquid. Allow full marks for a correctly labelled diagram.

2 Graph with sensible scales on axes (1) and axes labelled. (1) All points correctly plotted to ± half a square. (1) Smooth curve passing through all the points except the anomalous result. (1)

  Anomalous result identified (1 min, –6 °C). (1)

CP12b & c Part 2

1 Your own results.
2 Your own results.
3 Your own results.
4 Your own results.

5 To stop the polystyrene cup falling over.

6 Polystyrene is a better insulating material than glass, so less energy from the warm water will be transferred to the surroundings.

7 The beaker would have allowed more energy from the water to be transferred to the surroundings, so it would look as if more energy was needed to raise the temperature of the water, and the value of the specific heat capacity calculated would be too high.

8 Suggestions for systematic errors could include a faulty thermometer, balance or joulemeter. Suggestions for random errors include not reading the instruments correctly.

Edexcel GCSE (9–1)
Combined Science — Answers

Exam-style questions

1. Specific heat capacity is the amount of energy needed to raise the temperature of 1 kg of a substance by 1 °C. (1)
2. **a** $11\,000 = 0.25 \times c \times 10$ (1)
   $c = 11\,000 / 2.5$ (1)
   $c = 4400$ J/kg °C (1)
   b Heat lost to the surroundings during the experiment (1) would increase energy required to raise the temperature of the water (1) so the calculated value for the specific heat capacity would be too high. (1)
   c Increase insulation to reduce heat loss. (1)

CP13a

1. Your own table.
2. Your own graph.
3. Answer will depend on your springs.
4. Your own results.
5. The springs with the largest spring constants should feel the stiffest.
6. Your own results.

Exam-style questions

1. **a** two similarities such as: (2)
   - both use the same load
   - both start / end with same extension
   - both return to original length

   two differences such as: (2)
   - extensions for spring and rubber band differ
   - spring – loading and unloading are the same, rubber band – different
   - extension – spring linear, rubber band non-linear

   b i spring constant = 20 N/0.5 m (1) = 40 N/m (1)
   ii energy transferred = 0.5×40 N/m $\times (0.5$ m$)^2$ (1) = 5 J (1)

2. **a** If the total extension is 1 cm, the change with each weight added will be very small (1), and it will be difficult to get an accurate measurement of the extension for each weight. (1) (Similar explanations are acceptable.)
   b Use heavier weights (1), so the total extension is greater. (1)